A Long Tradition

The 9th (Airborne) Field Company, Royal Engineers at Arnhem

John Sliz

TRAVELOGUE 219

Copyright © 2011 Travelogue 219
All rights reserved. No part of this book may be reproduced, stored in a retrieval system, or transmitted in any form without the written permission of the publisher.

MGES-6 A Long Tradition: The 9th (Airborne) Field Company, Royal Engineers At Arnhem Edition 1.2 September 2011
Published by: Travelogue 219
            Toronto, Canada
ISBN 978-0-9877404-4-1

All Maps, Charts and Drawings by John Sliz

Front cover photos: No. 3 Platoon in Italy. (Philip Reinders)

Thank you to Barry Dougherty, Philip Reinders, Geert Maassen and Laura Sliz.

It is my best intention to honour the men of the 9th (Airborne) Field Company, R.E. by accurately recording their accomplishments. If you think that I have misquoted anyone, gotten anything wrong or have more information please let me know via my website.

visit: www.stormboatkings.ca

Contents

Glossary.. iv
Introduction.. 1
A Brief History.. 2
Operation Market Garden.. 7
Monday 18th September.. 20
Siege Part I.. 26
Sapper Task... 39
Siege Part II.. 40
Withdrawal.. 43
After Arnhem... 48
After Word.. 49
End Notes... 51
Roll Of Honour... 55
Roll: 9th (Airborne) Field Company, Royal Engineers........ 58
References.. 61
Index... 62
About The Author... 63

Maps

Operation Market Garden.. 6
1st Airborne Division's Landing And Drop Zones................. 8
The Sonnenberg Defences.. 25
The Road Bridge... 27
Last Positions.. 31
The Oosterbeek Perimeter.. 46

Glossary

AA	Anti-aircraft
Abn	Airborne
ADS	Advanced Dressing Station
A.R.P.	Fire extinguisher
Bn.	Battalion
Bren	British machine gun.
Class 9	A designation for a bridge that can take loads up to and including 9 tons. ie, most medium trucks and cars
CO	Commanding officer
Comns	Communication
Coy	Company
Cpl.	Corporal
CRE	Commander Royal Engineers
CSM	Company Sergeant Major
Cwt	Hundredweight
Div	Division
DUKW	An amphibious truck
DZ	Drop zone
Est	Establish
FBE	Folding Boat Equipment mostly used for bridging, but was able to transport infantry
Fd Pk	Field Park
FOO	Field Observation Officer of the Royal Artillery
GSO	General Staff Officer
HQ	Headquarters
Hrs	Hours
Indp	Independent
L/Cpl	Lance Corporal
Lt	Lieutenant
LZ	Landing zone
MC	Military Cross
MG	Machine Gun
MM	Military Medal
MMG	Medium machine gun
MT	Motor Transport
NCO	Non-commissioned officer
O-Group	A meeting of commanders
O.P.	Observation Post
Op	Operation
O.R.	Other Ranks
PIAT	Projector, Infantry, Anti-tank
POW	Prisoner Of War
QM	Quarter-master
RAP	Regimental Aid Post
RAF	Royal Air Force
RAMC	Royal Army Medical Corps
Recce	Reconnaissance
RE/R.E.	Royal Engineers
RV	Rendezvous
Sapper	The equivalent to a Private in the Engineer Corps
2i/c 2IC	Second in command
SP	Self-propelled gun
Spr	Sapper
USAAF	United States Army Air Force
Wrls	Wireless
X	Cross. Usually means crossroads

Introduction

This work is a snapshot of one of the engineer units that took part in Operation Market Garden, the 35,000 man airborne assault into The Netherlands to capture a series of bridges that would lead around the West Wall and into the heart of Germany. If all had gone well, Montgomery's 21st Army Group probably would have beaten the Russians to Berlin and ended the war before Christmas 1944. This epic battle has been told many times from an overall view and has been the subject of many debates as to why the operation failed. This won't be repeated here. Instead, I offer a worm's eye view of a small, specialized group of men who did everything that was asked of them and more; all with the bare amount of equipment and supplies.

Most of the plans for the 9th went awry right from the start, forcing them to improvise and spend most of their time fighting as infantry. As circumstances dictated, no other engineer company in the 1st Airborne Division was spread out as much as the 9th or had a higher percentage of men killed. They also were in every major action during the Battle Of Arnhem, fighting from the landing zone to the Arnhem road bridge, losing forty-five men killed in the process; eight of which have no known grave.

Compiled from personal accounts, war diaries, reports and a selected bibliography, this is the story of the 9th Field Company, Royal Engineers (R.E.) during the nine days of Operation Market Garden.

A Brief History

The 9th Field Company, Royal Engineers can trace their roots back to 1787 when it was first raised as the Chatham Company in the Corps of Royal Military Artificers. At the time it consisted of a hundred men of all ranks who were mostly employed on construction work. In September 1806, reorganization took place where the companies were redesignated numerically rather than by name. The Chatham Company became the 2nd Company and its strength was increased by twenty-six men. In August 1811 it was again renamed and became known as the 1st Company of the 2nd Battalion.

In May 1817 the company landed in Gibraltar and within two years was renamed the 9th Company of the Royal Sappers of Miners. Their new name reflected the type of work that they had been doing whilst on The Rock. For two years they were very busy tunneling a vast network of tunnels, chambers, stairs and galleries before they left in June 1827. From 1833 to 1842, on the Island of Corfu, the company worked on a citadel and other defenses.

The 9th was heavily involved in the Kaffir Wars in South Africa that lasted between 1846 to 1895. During this time, the company was rarely used as artisans and were involved mostly in keeping the peace between various tribes and the Dutch settlers. It left in July 1853 for the U.K. where it stayed until 1855 before leaving for the Crimean War. During that war they were put into the line and immediately started to improve the defenses. Unfortunately, this was not done without casualties. During this period the first use of Anti-Personnel mines was first recorded. The battered and greatly depleted 9th left the Crimean in May 1856, making them one of the last sapper units to leave.

Back on Corfu Island they built roads and defenses until early 1861. A year later the company sailed for Bermuda. There they built a large fort on Somerset Island. In October 1869 the 9th landed in Halifax and worked on a railway between the St. Lawrence River and the port of Halifax.

Now known as the 9th Fortress Company, Royal Engineers, they landed in Glasgow in 1876 and spent two years there before returning to Chatham. They served in Gibraltar from 1880 to 1886, Hong Kong in 1887 and then finally returned back to Chatham in 1891. At this time, the company was renamed the 9th Field Company, Royal Engineers.

The Boer War was their next stop. They sailed in January 1900 as part of the 7th Division South African Field Force. By March the 9th were transferred to Corps Troops and consisted of 7 officers and 161 other ranks, along with 14 horses and an assortment of oxen, mules and carts. Its duties were construction of defenses, railway bridges and the building of a hospital. They remained in South Africa long after the final peace agreement and built blockhouses and destroyed farm houses of suspected commando groups. They returned home in early 1905.

During World War I the 9th was part of the 4th Division and during the initial retreat blew up several bridges, losing its CO in the process. After much fighting the 9th returned to Britain in 1919, where it was reformed and re-equipped before it went to Germany to be part of the British Army of the Rhine. They served there until 1924.

At the time of the outbreak of World War II the 9th was still part of the 4th Division, but it was soon attached to the 48th Division to be part of the British Expeditionary Force. In a role reminiscent of the start of World War I the company was involved in a fighting retreat, but fortunately this time they didn't lose its CO while doing so. The 9th was evacuated just two days before the end of the Dunkirk evacuation.

To counter the possible German invasion the 9th was ordered to Plymouth. They soon found themselves clearing bomb damage, shoring up buildings and defusing unexploded bombs.

The 9th was selected to become the first field company in the Airborne forces and the ill-fated Operation Freshman was to be its first mission. Launched on 19 November 1942, two gliders carrying men of the 9th were on a mission to blow up the Norsk Hydro plant in Norway. This factory was suspected in the making of deuterium oxide (more commonly known as heavy water) that was used in making an Atomic bomb. Unfortunately, the operation didn't go as planned and all thirty-four occupants of both the gliders either died on landing or were executed by the Germans.

The invasion of Sicily was also not without its problems and those affecting the 9th resulted in numerous glider crashes. Some were shot down by friendly fire from the Allied navy and some were victims of inexperienced air crews. However, despite the setbacks the objectives were taken.[1] Unfortunately, Major Beasley was killed in Syracuse. His replacement was his second in command, Robert McNeile.[2]

A Long Tradition

The U.S.S. Boise took them to Taranto, Italy where they performed dock operations and the running of a supply column to the forward areas. Later, they moved forward with the 1st Airlanding Brigade and supported them.

The 9th was home by Christmas and was based in Lincolnshire with its headquarters in Tattershall.

By the summer Major J.C. Winchester was the commanding officer, with Captain P.H. Wetherill as his second in command and Lieutenant E.G. Wise as the Intelligence Officer. Number One Platoon was commanded by Captain R.B. Binyon, Number Two Platoon was under Captain E.C. O'Callaghan and Number Three Platoon by Captain M. Heggie.³

The 1942 War Establishment of the Airborne Field Company, R.E. was two hundred and forty-one men of all ranks, including 9 officers. Each platoon was made up of a small headquarters with two Jeeps and trailers for carrying stores and equipment, and three sections of twelve men each. Each platoon had two #22 radio sets, two radio operators, forty-seven bicycles and eight motorcycles, two of which had sidecars. However, not all the vehicles would go with them to Arnhem. Some of the transport went with the Seaborne Tail.⁴

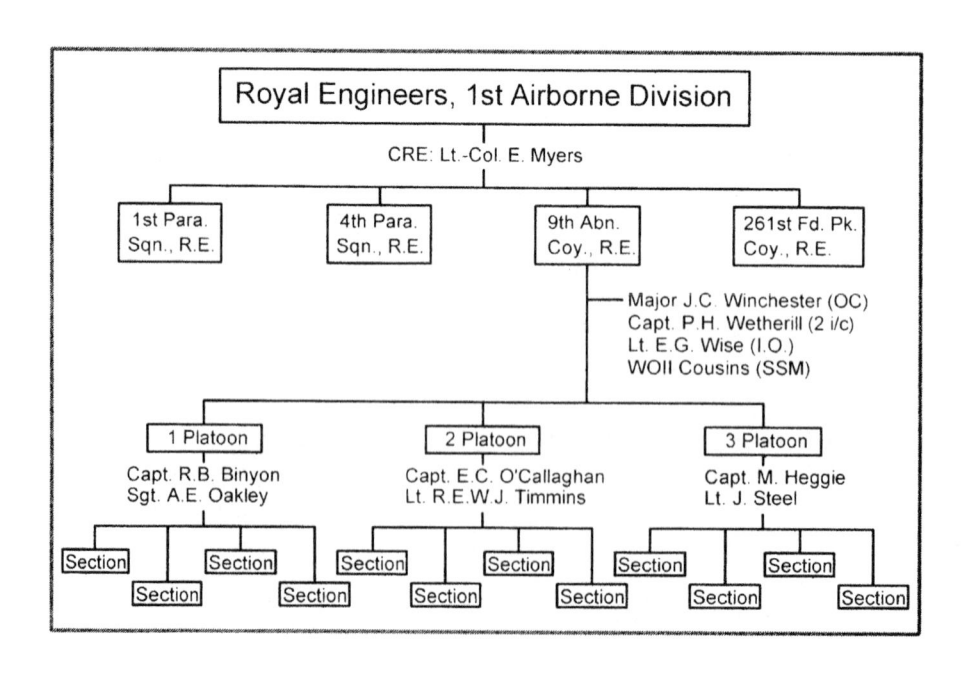

```
                Royal Engineers, 1st Airborne Division
                       CRE: Lt.-Col. E. Myers
    ┌──────────────┬──────────────┬──────────────┐
 1st Para.      4th Para.      9th Abn.       261st Fd. Pk.
 Sqn., R.E.     Sqn., R.E.     Coy., R.E.     Coy., R.E.

                                Major J.C. Winchester (OC)
                                Capt. P.H. Wetherill (2 i/c)
                                Lt. E.G. Wise (I.O.)
                                WOII Cousins (SSM)

        ┌───────────────┬───────────────┐
    1 Platoon       2 Platoon       3 Platoon
   Capt. R.B. Binyon  Capt. E.C. O'Callaghan  Capt. M. Heggie
   Sgt. A.E. Oakley   Lt. R.E.W.J. Timmins    Lt. J. Steel

  Section Section   Section Section   Section Section
    Section Section   Section Section   Section Section
```

Above: Third Platoon in Italy.
(Philip Reinders)

Two members of the company.
Above left: I. Hannabus of No. 3 Platoon. He was one of the few that returned from the operation.
Above right: Corporal William Barber of No.1 Platoon. He spent the rest of the was as a POW.
(both pictures courtesy of Philip Reinders)

A Long Tradition

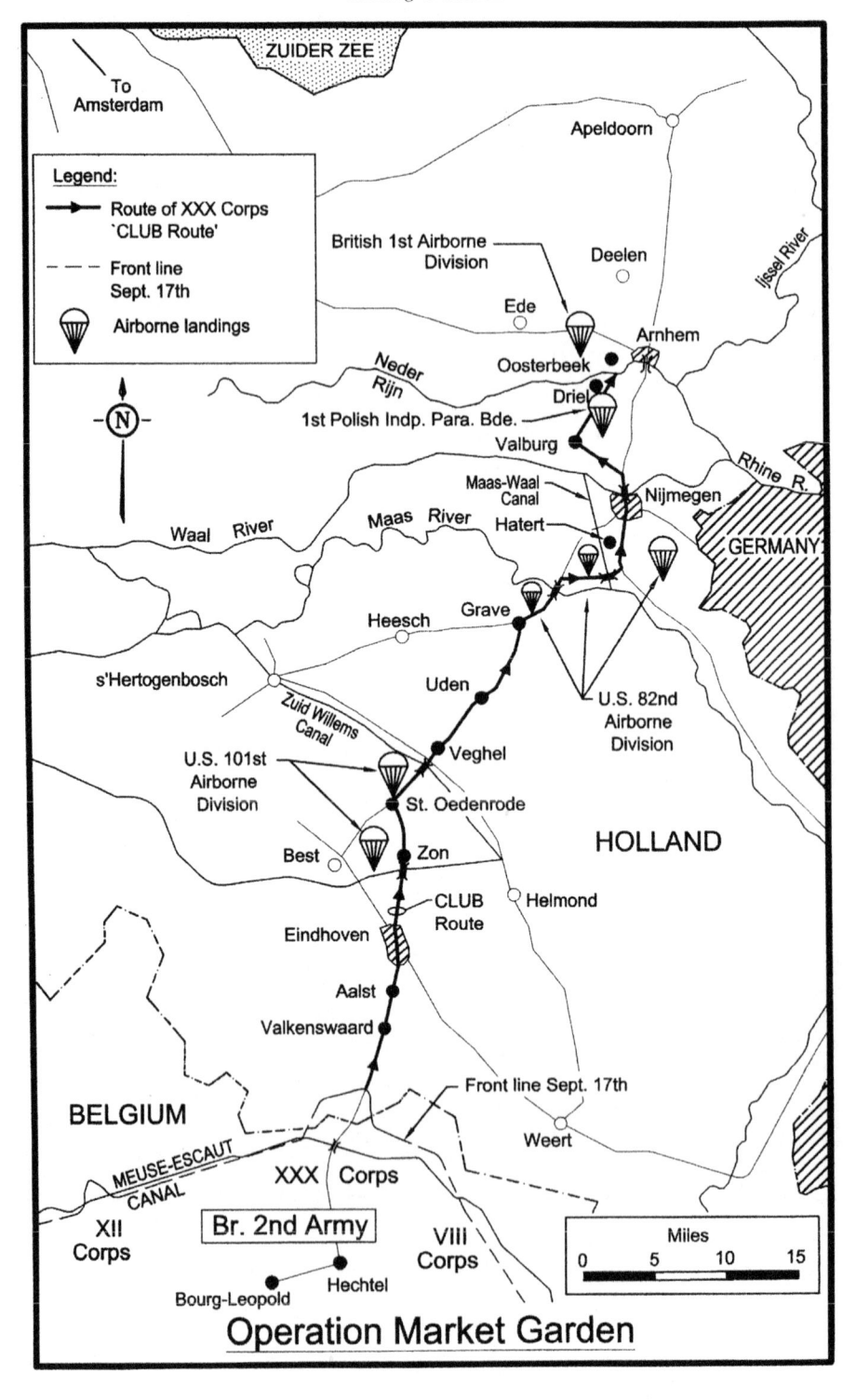

Operation Market Garden

Operation Market Garden

I will let Major J. C. Winchester outline the tasks of his company. The CRE was Colonel Edmund Myers. He said, *"For Operation MARKET the CRE had given my company, 9 (Airborne) Fd Coy, the following tasks. First, I had to provide two similar detachments, each of an officer and two jeep loads of sappers and equipment (provided by 3 Platoon), to accompany the Recce Sqn, which had been ordered to make a dash for the main ARNHEM road bridge immediately after landing. Secondly, I was to put one platoon (I detailed 1 Platoon), with a Clarke Crawler and detachment from 261 Fd Pk Coy, under command 1 Airlanding Brigade to assist in clearing the LZ of vehicles, until further engineer tasks became more definite. Thirdly, I had to provide a force to seize and hold the railway bridge over the R NEDER RIJN at 706763. No infantry had been detailed for this task, so I ordered the whole of 2 Platoon to take it on. The remainder of the company - Company HQ and half of 3 Platoon - was to RV at TAFELLAAN 718792. I was told that I might have to recce and possibly operate ferries across the NEDER RIJN with men from this last party. In fact the whole company was committed to definite tasks on landing."* [5]

The ferries that he mentioned were to be operated between the railway bridge and the pontoon bridge. No mention of the Heavendorp ferry appears anywhere in the CRE orders for the division's engineers.[6]

For the operation the company was allocated nineteen gliders with a further two for elements of the 261st Airborne Field Park Company that was attached. Sixteen of these were scheduled to land on the first day and five more were to land on the following day. I am unsure of the loading of every glider as the chart attached to the War Dairy is clearly wrong in spots. There seems to be a reshuffling of loads that wasn't updated on the chart. This was probably done while the gliders were loaded two days previously.[7]

Reveille was at 0500 hours on Sunday the 17th of September and after they checked their equipment, handed in their sleeping bags, had an early breakfast, checked weapons and drew ammunition, they boarded the trucks to take them to their gliders.[8]

As the men waited in the gliders the general consensus was that the operation was going to be cancelled like it had been, par for the course for the last few months. However, the cancel order never came and instead the men heard the Major bang on the

Landing Schedule

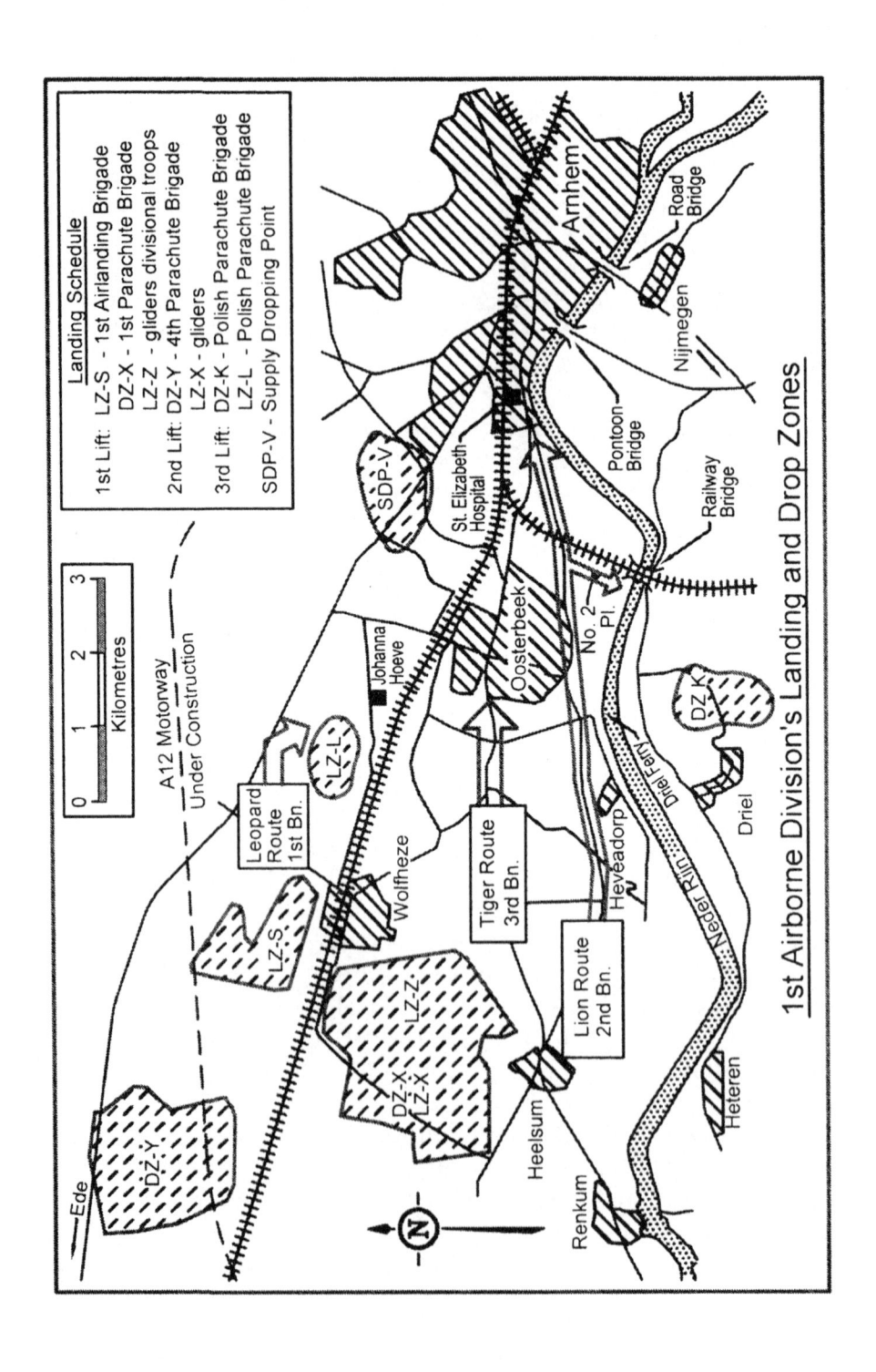

1st Lift: LZ-S - 1st Airlanding Brigade
DZ-X - 1st Parachute Brigade
LZ-Z - gliders divisional troops
2nd Lift: DZ-Y - 4th Parachute Brigade
LZ-X - gliders
3rd Lift: DZ-K - Polish Parachute Brigade
LZ-L - Polish Parachute Brigade
SDP-V - Supply Dropping Point

1st Airborne Division's Landing and Drop Zones

side of the glider and say, *"Chaps, we're on our way. See you over there. Good luck."* This electrified Sapper Tom Carpenter of No. 2 Platoon. *`At last it was on and they were about to land behind enemy lines."* [9]

Starting at 1020 hours on Sunday 17 September, sixteen Stirlings from 299 Squadron RAF took off from Keevil airfield towing sixteen Horsa gliders and joined the growing formation that was heading towards The Netherlands. The gliders were flown by the members of 21 Flight, D Squadron, Glider Pilot Regiment. The majority of these gliders carried the 9th Field Company, Royal Engineers, but one glider was from the REHQ and a second glider carried a detachment of the 261st Field Park on board.[10]

Sapper Carpenter, *"...we were gathering speed along the runway, there was a calm lulling motion as we became airborne. There was hardly any wind on this beautiful sunny Sunday morning as we gradually gained altitude and looking out of our small portholes we could soon see the Bristol Channel below."* [11]

As pleasant as that sounds, not all gliders made it past that point. Sergeant Wally Simpson was the tail gunner of the Flying Officer Geoff Liggins' Stirling and was watching glider #390* trailing behind. They were still over England when Sergeant Simpson recalled, *"suddenly the glider just seemed to part in the middle, it looked as if the tail portion parted from the front. Horrified, I shouted to the skipper, `My God, the glider is coming apart'".*[12]

The airman watched the tail section fall downwards while the front section that was still attached via tow rope was falling as well. The weight of the glider snapped the tow rope from the Stirling. Sergeant Simpson, *"Had the tow rope not broken when it did I shudder to think what might have been. It all happened so quickly. Even if we had been able to release the glider, I still doubt to this day if the mechanism would have functioned correctly due to the weight and angle of the glider."* [13]

One of the ground crew, Flight Sergeant K. Crowther, was one of those who witnessed the tragic accident. He saw the tail break away and the glider plunge to the ground. He knew that there was little hope that anyone had survived the fall.[14]

Flying Officer Liggins broke formation and flew over the crash site, noting the location. Later, he and his crew took a jeep

---

*some reports and books have this as glider#389. The War Diary and the men of the Stirling that was towing it say that it was #390 so I will go with that.

to view what was left of the glider. Sergeant Simpson described it, *"like a matchbox that had been stepped on."* [15]

The RAF report stated that it was an accident due to structural damage.[16]

Another glider didn't make it, but fortunately its flight was a lot less dramatic. The Stirling towing glider #383 had engine trouble and it had to turn back. It released the glider over the airfield and both made a good landing.[17]

Enroute a third glider had its problems. After flying for two hours Glider #385, containing a jeep and a trailer, was caught in a slipstream that forced its tug to go into a spiral dive. The rope pulled off at a thousand feet. Driver R. Jardine of Company Headquarters was in the glider. He said, *"...some time after take off we crash landed in a field in England and were soon surrounded by Home Guard. I think we might have been in the region of St. Albans. After a Sergeant Major of the local Home Guard took us to their mess tent and gave us a bottle of beer each, they helped us unload the glider and we set off back to Keevil where we were allocated another glider. We reloaded and this time we made it to Arnhem with the next lift."* [18]

The remaining gliders were now part of a mass armada headed for The Netherlands. Sapper Carpenter, *"We were now over the North Sea and looking down from about 3000 feet, it looked like a millpond and very calm, we could see rescue ships, some already dealing with ditched and ditching gliders. There was to be no Sicily fiasco this time as we approached the Dutch coastline. Black puffs of smoke appeared as flack ships tried to get our range. Then the sad sight as vast stretches of flooded lowland slipped beneath us with the occasional rooftop barely visible, a very sobering sight. Everyone around me now started checking his personal equipment and weapons again as we neared our landing zone."* [19]

At approximately 1340 hours the gliders carrying the 9th started to land on LZ `Z'. Of the thirteen remaining gliders only one didn't have a safe landing. As glider # 386 approached the landing zone, Major Winchester peered over the pilot's shoulder, looking for land marks or anything that could impede the Company's progress. Then the glider cast off its tow line, decelerating rapidly before going into its characteristic steep dive. The two pilots had to make an instantaneous appraisal of the best location to put the glider down, but the Horsa hit the ground to the sounds of splintering wood as the undercarriage burst through the floor. Sapper Holdstock, the OC's radio operator, was thrown

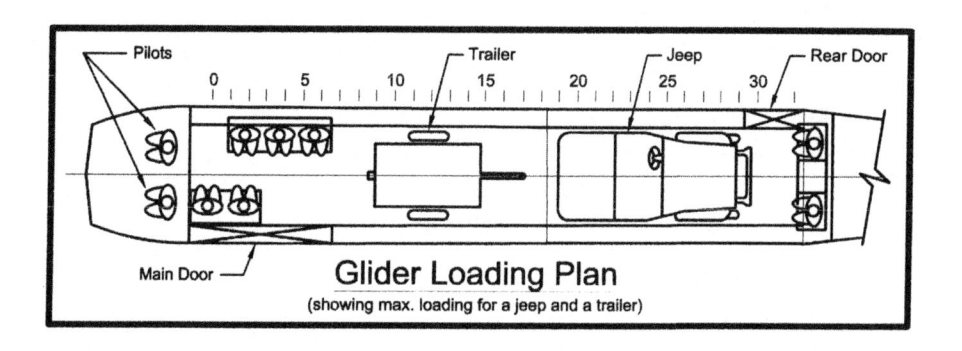

Glider Loading Plan
(showing max. loading for a jeep and a trailer)

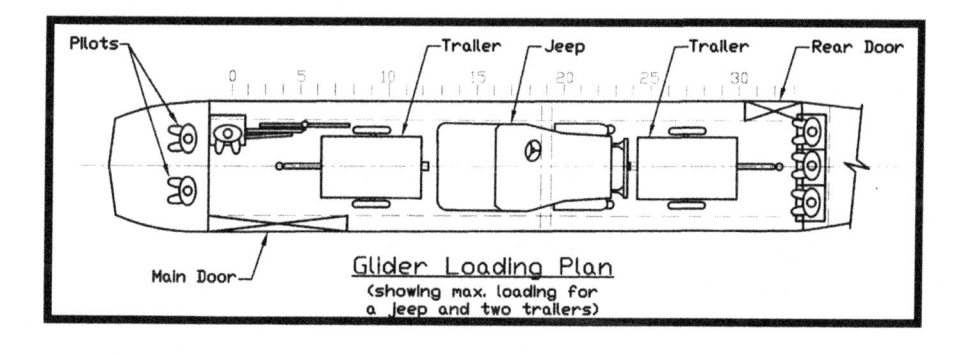

Glider Loading Plan
(showing max. loading for a jeep and two trailers)

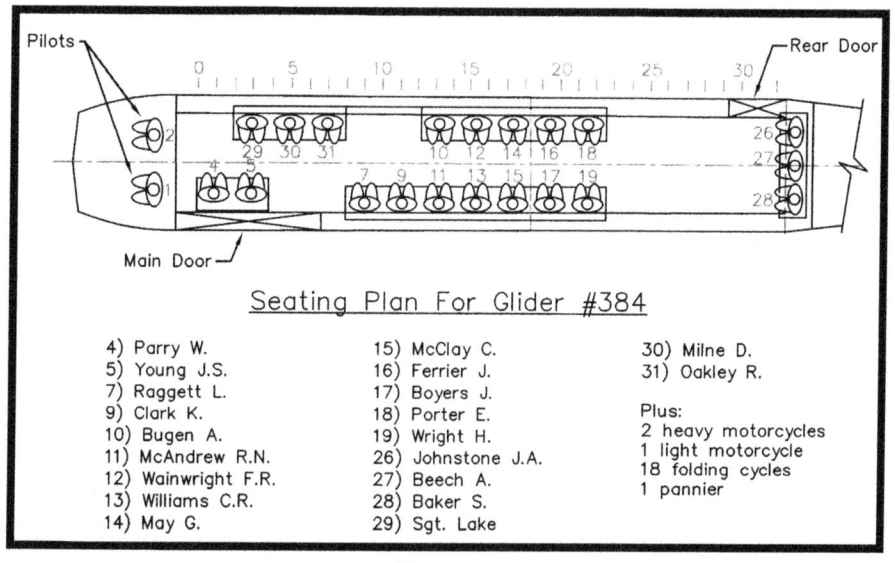

Seating Plan For Glider #384

4) Parry W.
5) Young J.S.
7) Raggett L.
9) Clark K.
10) Bugen A.
11) McAndrew R.N.
12) Wainwright F.R.
13) Williams C.R.
14) May G.

15) McClay C.
16) Ferrier J.
17) Boyers J.
18) Porter E.
19) Wright H.
26) Johnstone J.A.
27) Beech A.
28) Baker S.
29) Sgt. Lake

30) Milne D.
31) Oakley R.

Plus:
2 heavy motorcycles
1 light motorcycle
18 folding cycles
1 pannier

from the glider, sustaining injuries from which he later died. Sergeant Paffet and Sapper Robertson both received leg and ankle injuries. The pilots and the rest of those on board were shaken, but recovered.[20]

Sapper A.T. Williams of No. 1 Platoon tells of a more pleasant landing. *"We had a safe landing and the Glider pilots put the glider exactly where they wanted. Then we knocked the end off the glider and unloaded the jeep and bicycles and were ready in minutes. Dutch people came to us with bottles of wine and other things. It was almost too easy. We set off on our bikes to the rendezvous with our gear but I realized we were sitting targets on those bikes and decided to leave them in a ditch."*[21]

The Company's rendezvous was the southeast corner of LZ 'Z' and by 1415 hours the company had assembled. Major Winchester assessed the situation, *"2 Platoon (Captain O'Callaghan) had landed complete, reported, and was on its way to the railway bridge. 1 Platoon (Captain Binyon), which was in support of 1 Airlanding Brigade, had lost one complete glider of 23 sappers, which had blown up in the air en route. One of the detachments from 3 Platoon (Captain Heggie), which had been detailed to accompany the Recce Sqn, failed to arrive, so a second detachment was hastily organized and sent off in its place. Company HQ landed complete except for a few casualties in my glider."* [22]

The Company's first headquarters was to be in the Wolfhezen hotel, which the Major had selected from aerial photographs, so shortly after landing the Intelligence Officer, Lieutenant Wise, set out with Sapper Raymond H. Foster, Driver Fairs, Sappers Beaver and Greig in a jeep with a trailer to recce the route to the hotel. They came to a road junction and saw an old black car with a red cross on it. Foster covered the other four as they got out of the jeep to have a look around. Wise called out, *"Steady"* and was about to open the car door when the enemy opened up. There was a burst of a machine gun and fire from about two to three snipers. Lieutenant Wise was hit in the thigh, Sapper Beaver in the face and Greig was very badly wounded. When two men tried to get Greig to bring him back they were also hit. Lieutenant Wise and his party managed to retreat.[23]

A different account has Lieutenant Wise only with Sergeant Miller, who were still in the jeep when the Germans opened up on them. The Lieutenant was hit in both legs and in the left arm with a piece of metal that ripped his nose open. The same account also has Sapper Greig being hit later on while with Lieutenant Timmins.[24]

The Lieutenant was able to walk, albeit slowly, and reported back to the Major. He and the other wounded were rushed to the First Aid Post in a jeep that had the radio for headquarters. Sapper Shepard, the radio operator, said that this action left him without a job to do. As he put it, *"Everything went terribly wrong, first we were issued with the wrong radio crystals from the Royal Army Ordnance Corps who had all the stores, so in effect the 22 sets were non-operational though we did not know this yet."* [25]

At 1430 hours Captain Heggie, now at half strength, with two jeeps and eleven men left the company rendezvous to join the Recce Squadron at their rendezvous. Unfortunately, the *coup de main* party was already heading towards the Arnhem Road Bridge along the Leopard route. According to John Fairley, a member of the Recce Squadron, the four jeeps that were supposed to accompanied them on their *coup de main* never arrived. He blames an organizational flaw and not the units involved and wrote, *"The gliders that carried Captain Heggie and his men weren't sent in the flight serials next to the Squadron nor even in the same zone. This alone was enough cause for an unnecessary delay and for a group that had a task where every second was vital, waiting for a team from another field was out of the question. This simple organizational oversight resulted in the engineers not linking up with the coup de main party."* The Captain did find part of the Recce Squadron at the rendezvous and stayed with them on the landing zone.[26]

At 1500 hours Captain O'Callaghan and No. 2 Platoon, less one section, left the Company R.V. to capture the railway bridge. No. 1 Platoon was under the command of 1st Airlanding Brigade and, as the infantry were clearing Wolfhezen, they wanted the 1st Platoon to catch any stragglers. In addition, Major Winchester, acting on this information from Lieutenant Wise, ordered Captain Binyon and his platoon to clear the route to, and occupy, the Wolfhezen Hotel." [27]

What he didn't know was that Lieutenant Wise and his party had bumped into Number 2 Company, SS Panzer Grenadier Depot and Reserve Battalion 16, commonly known as Battalion Krafft after its commander Strumbannfuhrer Josef Krafft. Its strength at the time was three hundred and six men, but they weren't fully trained. However, they were in the right location at the right time. In fact, Number 2 Company was in the woods that morning for a training exercise. Battalion Krafft formed a north-south blocking line just east of Wolfhezen that covered the railway line and the Utrecht road with his headquarters in the Wolfhezen hotel.[28]

Running into this line, Captain Binyou and 1st Platoon were held up in the hotel grounds. Sapper A.T. Williams, *"During the way we met opposition of a German patrol in the woods and we got far as the edge. Somebody opened fire and we, a group of seven men, opened fire back. This was the first opposition we had."* [29]

With No. 2 Platoon elsewhere and No. 1 Platoon held up, Major Winchester only had a section from No. 2 Platoon and half of No. 3 Platoon to help capture the Wolfhezen hotel. He sent No. 3 Platoon and around 1545 hours they were held up by machine gun fire coming from the southeast. Lieutenant J. Steel, the 2 i/c of 3rd Platoon halted the column and went forward to scout the area. He was not heard from again.[30]

At 1800 hours, under command of Lieutenant R.E.W.J. Timmins, No. 5 Section was sent away to recce the route to the hotel in Wolfhezen through the woods. Sapper E. Thorne, *"I was walking ahead. Lieutenant Timmins behind me and another scout on the right of me, the rest of the section was behind Timmins. We had turned left as we came near a crossing point; at the moment we turned left a German machine gun opened fire. When I heard the machine gun I dropped to the ground and saw Timmins was shot through the chest and fell to the ground. He told me 'Get back if you can, get back!' The other scout knew there was no need to come up and had gone back to the rest of the Company, the rest of No. 5 section had already got back. I was left on my own and spent the night in the woods. The next morning I met a Royal Artillery Officer and we decided to bury Lieutenant Timmins at the place where he was killed."* This was a hundred metres west of the Wolfhezen Hotel. In the action, L/Cpl. William Takle was severely wounded. He died the next day. This was also the same action where some accounts say that Sapper Grieg was wounded.[31]

Around 1800 hours, Lieutenant-Colonel Myers ordered Major Winchester to occupy a defensive position within half a mile of the LZ to protect the Royal Artillery's southern flank. The Major ordered Captain Binyon's platoon to withdraw. Company HQ and No. 3 Platoon dug in, protecting the guns at the tracks five hundred yards east of the original rendezvous. Around 1900 hours the south corner of the company's defenses were attacked by a stray enemy party with a machine gun. Three enemy were

Above: The viaduct under the railroad embankment looking east. It was here that No. 2 Platoon left their jeep and bicycles in preparation of heading south towards the railroad bridge.
(taken by Author)

Left: Sapper Tom Carpenter of No. 2 Platoon.
(photo courtesy of Philip Reinders)

killed and an estimated another three wounded. The machine gun was captured and the dead were identified as Hitler Jugend.

The orders to withdraw didn't reach 1st Platoon until roughly 1930 hours and Captain Binyon ordered his platoon and Lieutenant Timmins' section back to the main company position.[32]

Meanwhile No. 2 Platoon had been advancing towards the railway bridge. Captain O'Callaghan left his jeep and trailer under the viaduct under the railroad embankment and ordered the men to pile their bikes there as well. They prepared to attack and set off along the western side of the embankment under the cover of bushes. They passed the abandoned train and they knocked out an anti-aircraft position.

Captain O'Callaghan, *"Around 1800 hours we attacked the railway bridge along the embankment whilst a platoon from C Company, 2nd Parachute Battalion attacked it from the line of the river bank. Reached objective within 30 minutes, opposition slight, the enemy withdrawing to far bank very quickly. As both assaults reached the bridge, the centre span was blown up. There was fire coming from the far bank and two houses quite near it. The Para Platoon Commander was wounded and another Para killed whilst I was making a recce of the riverbank for a crossing."* [33]

A few men checked the rest of the bridge for explosives and found none while the others set up a defensive position around the embankment. The Captain radioed headquarters, "Objective lost, seek further instructions." [34]

Captain O'Callaghan, *"Sapper Tom Hyland, my wireless operator, could not contact the company.* Lieutenant-Colonel John Frost ordered me to search the bridge for any further charges, this I did as best as I could but the enemy fire made things very difficult. I finished my search of the bridge, finding no further charges, decided to push on to the pontoon bridge where I could get instructions from the Officer Commanding C Company. But Major V. Dover had moved away by now, so I withdrew from the bridge and reorganized on the main road. 1st Parachute Brigade Headquarters passed by and the brigade Major, Major J.A. Hibbert told me to join his column."* [35]

This action goes against the CRE orders of which No. 2 Platoon was under control. They were not under 1st Parachute Brigade's command at the time and should have stayed at the railway bridge. The brigade already had most of the 1st Parachute

---

*The only frequency that he could get with any degree of consistency was the BBC. [36]

Squadron, Royal Engineers with them and that was more than sufficient for the little engineering tasks available. In the Captain's defense, his platoon's task at the railway bridge was completed. His orders read that one detachment will seize and hold the railway bridge and remove all demolition charges, and make temporary cut of the railway tracks from the south. By blowing the centre span, the Germans effectively did his job for him. All he had to do was to check to see if there were any more charges.

In a report called, 'Lessons From Arnhem' Colonel Myers called Captain O'Callaghan, *"...a particularly forceful and brave officer."* and stated that his *"decision to attempt to seize, without specific instructions, the pontoon bridge after having failed in his initial task, cannot be judged in the absence of all knowledge of the local situation."* [37]

Back at the road, they collected their bikes and according to Tom Carpenter, the Captain said, *"We're doing no bloody good here. We'll go for a stroll to Arnhem. It's just the day for it. Keep close, keep going. We're not going to get bogged down in a firefight. We'll just go for the bridge."* [38]

Getting through the viaduct under the railroad was a little difficult as the Germans on the other side of the river had zeroed in on the tunnel. Fortunately, the light was fading and the entire platoon made it through without injury. As the platoon started up the slope towards the hospital a Dutch resistance member informed them of the lower route that bypassed the centre of town where a lot of fighting was taking place.

Near the pontoon bridge a machine gun fired across a square at the platoon as they crossed. Fire also came from behind the column and it was quickly determined that machine gun fire was coming from several different sources. This is the same ambush that the 1st Parachute Squadron, R.E. and other groups had gone through earlier. It should have been taken care of earlier, but since everyone was in a mad rush to get to the bridge, it was ignored. A few men returned fire and the machine guns stopped. The bicycles were abandoned and the men crawled forward to safety. The Captain insisted that the jeep wasn't left behind so the driver made a dash for it and drove it to safety.

The platoon reached the pontoon bridge and saw that the middle section had been taken away. They also saw the bodies of four Germans. After searching for boats and finding that the centre section had been burnt and was quite useless, Major Murray (CO of 1st Parachute Squadron, R.E.) and Captain E. O'Callaghan decided that it was wiser to have all the sappers at the road bridge. At 2300 they left only a handful of men behind from the 1st and headed towards the road bridge.³⁹

Around midnight they came to another ambush. This one was near the old town gate of Sabelspoort. Again, fire was coming from several different sources. The platoon was spread along the Rijnkade, hiding behind whatever cover they could find when an explosion came from the bridge. Two sappers from the 1st Parachute Squadron, Royal Engineers had attacked the pillbox on the bridge with a flamethrower and had inadvertently set it on fire. This lit up the entire area and the men of No. 2 Platoon were exposed. Fortunately, a carrier came to their rescue as it started firing its Bren Gun at the machine guns. The thirty or so men ran towards a big house on the corner and kicked the front door in. They filled the well-furnished middle-class home at 27 Eusebuisplein and within minutes had prepared it for a defensive stand. This meant that they destroyed anything that could be shattered by a bullet. Windows and everything with glass was broken with their rifle butts, curtains were also ripped down so they didn't catch fire and the furniture was pushed against the walls for added protection and firing nests.⁴⁰

By the end of the day, the Major hadn't heard from two of his three platoon commanders, Captains O'Callaghan and Heggie, as there was no wireless contact with them. Of the eight officers that had landed with him, Lieutenant Timmins was dead, Lieutenant Wise was wounded and Lieutenant Steel was missing; his motor-cycle was found riddled with bullets. Company Headquarters, No. 1 Platoon, No. 2 Platoon's 5th Section and half of No. 3 Platoon were with him defending the Royal Artillery guns east of the LZ-Z. Major Winchester, *"During the night, we were sniped by various parties of the enemy that were making their way through the woods towards ARNHEM. We drove them off with no casualties to ourselves, and a bag of three dead enemy and one captured MG. All the dead enemy were very young SS troops."* ⁴¹

What he didn't know was that No. 2 Platoon was at the bridge and that Captain Heggie and his party never made it there. They were still on the landing zone.

The 9th command structure was severely weakened. Yes, Major Winchester and Captain Wethered were still in command of the company and Captain Binyon was in command of No. 1 Platoon, but his second in command, Sergeant Oakley, had been killed when his glider crashed, Captain O'Callaghan and most of his platoon was missing, the second in command of No 2 Platoon and 5 section OC were dead and both officers of No. 3 Platoon were missing. Major Winchester must not have felt particularly optimistic about things on that first night, especially after losing twenty-three men and the knowledge that he was going to lose more.

Above: The houses and businesses close to the road bridge looking eastward. The 9th came into this area on the morning of the 18th and occupied the house closest to the bridge (mid left of picture) and the building in the middle of the photograph.

Monday 18 September

Around 0100 hours, Captain O'Callaghan took Sappers Danny Weddell and Tom Carpenter with him to scout the ground between their current position and the bridge. He didn't like the location of the house and wanted to be closer to the bridge. By moving through the backyards, they climbed walls that were about seven feet high and after about eight of these they were within striking distance of the bridge. Seeing this, the Captain ordered Sapper Carpenter to return to tell Sergeant Gibbons to move up the rest of the platoon. As he led the platoon to its new position, Tom lost count of the number of walls and went over one wall too many. He said, *"I scrambled over a wall and in front of me was a Jerry. He was crouched down and luckily he had his back to me. I looked round and I thought, Christ where are the rest of the lads? I must have gone too far."* Fortunately, the old German surrendered and Tom marched him with his hands up back around the wall and into the coffin factory. The move into the houses along the Eusebiusplein between the bridge and the Kadestraat was complete by 0830 hours.[42]

The possibility of the road bridge being blown was a continual worry to Colonel Frost, even though he had been reassured that the heat of the fires would destroy any fuses already laid from the bridge to the town, and that the sappers had cut all the cables that could be found. However, no one was sure that all the lines had been cut because the fires prevented anyone from being able to get on the bridge itself to remove any charges that might be there.[43]

Captain O'Callaghan started around 0900 hours to search one side of the bridge for enemy wires and charges, whilst Captain T.J. Livesey (Commander B Troop, 1st Parachute Squadron) searched the piers at his side. It was tricky work because the other end of the bridge was in enemy hands and there was heavy 88mm fire coming from that side. There were also two trucks on fire in the middle of the bridge. After they searched the bridge, No. 2 Platoon went into reserve in `A' Company, 2nd Parachute Battalion positions which were in a number of houses around the bridge. [44]

At 0930* hours came the famous charge across the bridge by SS-Captain Uiktoreberhard Graebner and his Reconnaissance Battalion 9, consisting of twenty-two armoured vehicles. The general consensus is that the experienced Captain was counting on surprise and shock to defeat the airborne troops. This tactic had worked in Normandy and he counted on it working again, especially against lightly armed airborne troops. He sent his armour in first.

These armoured cars were from the 1st Company and consisted of three Sdfz 222 and two Sdfz 231, which zig-zagged through the defenses and mines at high speed, firing their weapons as they went. One of them – most likely one of the eight wheeled Sdfz 231 – hit a mine and, despite losing a wheel, managed to make it into north Arnhem. Next came the slower half-tracks, which the British unleashed their fire against and knocked out.

Captain O'Callaghan, *"Around 0930 hours three enemy cars attacked the bridge from the south supported by a few infantry; the leading car was knocked out by Anti-Tank gunfire by Major W.F. Arnold's (1st Airlanding Anti-Tank Battery) detachment, which had been with the battalion from the start. The attack failed and at around 1030 hours for the third time that morning the enemy was trying again to do something to our end of the bridge but whatever their plan was, it failed due to the small arms fire from our position."* [45]

After two hours, the attack was a disaster for the Germans. Their Recon Battalion commander was dead and most of the battalion had been destroyed.

During these attacks and the heavy mortaring afterwards, Sapper Robert Trouse was killed and L/Cpl Coward and Sapper Harry Thompson were seriously wounded by mortar fire. Sapper Harry Thompson was hit in the head and neck and had been pulled by Tom Carpenter into the factory that made clogs and coffins. With the mortars still landing all around, Tom placed Harry in a coffin for added protection. After the mortars had stopped he and the other wounded were taken to the R.A.P. During this, Harry was still conscious and temporarily paralyzed and the act of being placed in a coffin prematurely had a long term effect on him. He didn't know why he had nightmares about it until years later, when Tom told him the full story. [46]

Sapper Trouse has no known grave and Sapper Thompson gave this statement after returning to England, *"I was wounded at the same time as Sapper Trouse and we were taken to the R.A.P. together. Sapper Trouse died from his wounds in the*

---

*Some accounts say 0830 and this may be because of the time difference between British Standard time and Dutch time. In MGES-3 'Engineers At The Bridge' I have it as 0830 hours.

R.A.P. *early the next day. I was present in the R.A.P. when he died."* 47

Meanwhile, the rest of the company was far less busy. Major Winchester, *"Surprisingly, Monday was a relatively quiet day of waiting. The CRE decided to keep us where we were, as his reserve, until the course of events became little clearer. There was very little news at divisional HQ; the fighting had been very confused, and I still had no news of the detached portions of my company."* 48

During the morning, because there was no news from No. 2 Platoon, and since no officer was available, the Major ordered Corporal H. Pink to take his section and a few others and go to the Arnhem Bridge to remove the charges there. There were eighteen men in total and they were attached to the 2nd Battalion, South Staffordshire Regiment, who were to proceed to the bridge by following the Utrechtseweg. Since the infantry were on foot the sappers were told to leave their bicycles behind. The section was with `B' Company, who was in the lead.49

Sapper J. Cook was part of Corporal Pink's section and he remembers being sniped at incessantly on the way down to St. Elisabeth's Hospital. He saw jeeps with personnel streaming back towards Oosterbeek with badly injured men in the a jeep, whose drivers told them that they were never going to make it to the bridge. *"At this point all hell broke loose and we came under murderous machine gun fire, our section took cover in a ditch and heavy casualties ensued. I got flash-blinded and was hit in the face with metal fragments from a Bren gun, which had received a hit from a mortar bomb. The next thing I could remember was hearing a woman's voice and a young boy telling me to bend my head under a hand water pump whilst they washed my face and tried to extract pieces of metal out of my cheeks, eyelids and other parts of my face. Also my right hand was pouring blood having been peppered with bits of metal."* 50

The South Staffordshire Regiment pressed on but was stopped by the museum and all but a handful of sappers were not wounded. One of the casualties was Corporal Pink who was wounded in the face.

Beaten, what was left of the relief force made it back to Oosterbeek and formed Lonsdale Force, of which Corporal Pink and his reinforced section were part.

About 1100 hours, a visit from Colonel Myers informed the Major that the Recce Squadron operation against the main road bridge around the north of the town had been held up and that

Captain Heggie was still with the Recce Squadron, who were now defending part of the drop zone. Captain Heggie reported having no casualties. Lieutenant Wise and Sergeant Paffett were dispatched to the hospital in Wolfhezen, which was now clear of enemy and held by some Glider Pilots.

At 1430 hours, the three and a half hour delayed second lift arrived and in addition to the six gliders scheduled to arrive were the two gliders that had to turn back on the first day; one glider bringing one jeep and trailer of the *Coup de main* party and a detachment from the 261st Field Park Company complete with bulldozer. Lance Corporal Hallam, who was hurt by the tail of a glider during its unloading, was evacuated to hospital.[51]

Sapper Morris Knight of Company HQ and the other men in his glider were supposed to be with the *Coup de main* group in their dash for the road bridge, but because of their false start on the first day, they were a day late. Their landing was fine and they soon had the jeep out of the glider, which was loaded with the radio equipment and on the front had a twin `K Gun'. They were fired on by some Germans who were running in the opposite direction so Sapper Knight's finger was on the trigger. Two minutes later, *"...as we drove along a track next to a field with long grass, a young girl came dashing out of the tall grass and not only did we nearly run her over I very nearly opened fire on her, she had been collecting the parachutes from the landing zone. I was lucky enough to meet her after the war and she remembered the incident, and a few years later I was invited to her wedding where she wore a wedding dress made from the white parachutes she collected from the landing zone, it was a great day. I'm so glad I didn't open fire, as there was a lot of fire coming at us and things were a bit hairy at the time and things were very confused."* [52]

Since the rest of the company had moved on, they were told to report to the Hartenstein where headquarters had been set up and Colonel Myers needed the radio and jeep. The radio was taken out of the jeep and taken into the headquarters' building and Sapper Knight was ordered to dig a slit trench under some trees and await orders. Now, with no radio to operate, he had become a `runner'. *"When Col Eddie saw that I had dug in, he ordered me to get a hand held battery charger and try and wind some power into some of the radio batteries, I sat in my trench on and off for the next three days turning the handles on the charger trying to gain enough power into the batteries to help contact our forces on the other side of the river."* [53]

At 1615 hours, Company headquarters and the remainder of Nos. 1 and 3 Platoons moved off to a new location in Oosterbeek, half a mile northwest of Division headquarters. Just after starting No. 1 Platoon was detached to Wolfhezen to destroy twenty-two enemy guns captured there by 1 Airlanding Brigade. These guns were stored on the grounds of the lunatic asylum and since one gun was found to be booby-trapped, Lieutenant Moore of the 1st Airlanding Regiment, Royal Artillery came to the conclusion that they all were of no use and should be destroyed.[54]

Major Winchester, *"In the late afternoon, we moved with divisional HQ further towards ARNHEM and took up a position in the beech woods just North-West of HARTESTEIN, around SONNENBERG house. This position commanded a good field of fire to the North-West and afforded excellent cover. Its strength was amply illustrated in the subsequent days of fighting, as we were never forced to give a yard of ground."* [55]

According to Major Perkins of the 4th Parachute Squadron, R.E. the Sonnenburg was *"...a large rather Victorian looking house, four stories high, and facing NORTH WEST. The house and various outbuildings had been used as a German soldiers' billet. We found their remnants. There was a gap in the trees immediately in front of the house and it was possible to [command] most of the valley from the top story. The wood on the right extended up along side a track to the NORTH WEST and the wood on the left which was only 100-200 yards in depth went down to the main road."* [56]

At 1800 hours the company arrived in its new location and started to dig into its new defensive positions south of the house.

Field of Fire. Looking southwest from their position at the Sonnenberg, the open ground gave the advantage to the defender. The house in the distance is near the Utretchsweg. (taken by Author)

The Sonnenberg Defences

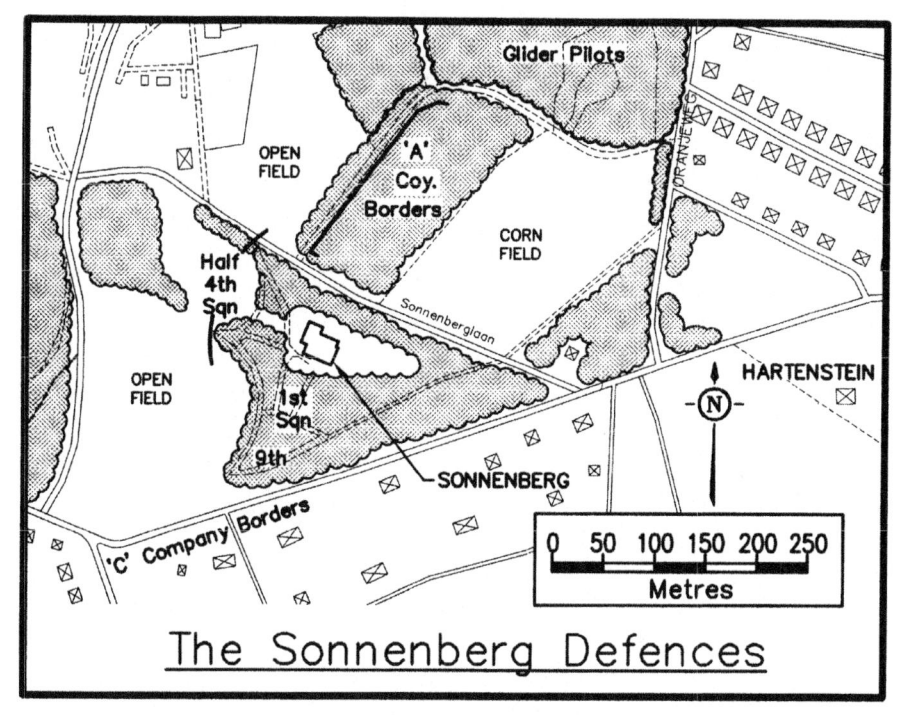

The wireless wasn't working correctly and had no contact except with CRE on #22 set. The Major still had no word from Captain O'Callaghan and No. 2 Platoon and Lieutenant Steel was still missing.[57]

Major Winchester, *"Monday night was noisy, but not unduly disturbing. We all dug fire positions most of the night and by the morning had good head cover of logs for all our slit trenches. Very little news of 2 and 3 Platoons came in, but I did hear that 2 Platoon had failed to get the railway bridge, which had been blown up in their faces. They had written off the enemy demolition party and then pushed on along the river bank further into ARNHEM, hoping to help in the capture of the main road bridge."* [58]

Lance Corporal Edwin Johnson, and a friend who he called 'Taffy', had crawled into the basement in total darkness to find somewhere to sleep. They found what they thought were some boxes and settled down inside them. In the morning, they awoke to find out that they were lying in coffins.[59]

On Monday, both L/Cpl William Tackle and Sapper Peter Grieg died of the wounds they had received yesterday. This brought the company's total for the day to three dead and twenty-six for the operation so far. That meant roughly one-eighth of the company that set out for Arnhem had been killed in just two days.

Siege Part I

During the morning of Tuesday the 19th, Captain Binyon and No. 1 Platoon finished the job they had started the day before by destroying twenty-two enemy guns in Wolfhezen with explosives. Then they proceeded to join the company at Sonnenberg.[60]

During the late morning, Major Winchester, Captain Heggie and a party of six sappers visited Heveadorp ferry and the jetty on the north bank approximately five hundred yards downstream with the objective of collecting diesel barges for future bridging operations. Major Winchester, *"On Tuesday morning, I reconnoitered the NEDER RIJN at HEVEADORP and found the flying ferry there in good condition and in operation. There were no enemy in the vicinity. We examined the river banks and found three diesel barges which we tried to get going without success. Two were stuck fast in the mud and the air bottle of the third, which was used for starting the engine, was exhausted."* [61]

One good thing about this recce trip was that Corporal Hey and two sappers brought in seven other ranks, mainly of South Staffordshire who had landed on the south side of the river.

The Major left a party behind under Sergeant Lake and returned to Company HQ just in time to assist in shooting up some enemy fighters that suddenly appeared and started strafing the divisional HQ area. The enemy fighters were engaged by light machine guns and small arms fire from all available weapons.[62]

Two Stirlings and three Dakotas were seen to be shot down during afternoon air re-supply. However, the company managed to collect a few panniers and according to the Major, *"food and ammunition were not short as yet and morale was very high."* [63]

Major Winchester, *"During the afternoon and evening, a party of about 70 sappers of 4 Para Sqn with Major Perkins and two other officers, and another party of about a dozen sappers from 1 Para Sqn under Captain George joined me in the SONNENBERG area. It had now been decided to concentrate the remains of the division in a perimeter around HARTENSTEIN. These sappers, with a platoon of infantry, were put under my command and I was made responsible for the defence of the North-West sector of the divisional perimeter. During the evening, my force was further reinforced with a 17 pounder anti-tank gun. We were now being mortared quite heavily and regularly, but by midnight we were all well dug-in and prepared to meet all comers."* [64]

Meanwhile at the bridge, three Mark III tanks were in a position where the anti-tank guns couldn't get at them and were attacking the school. Seeing this, Captain Tony Frank of `A'

2 Platoon Positions

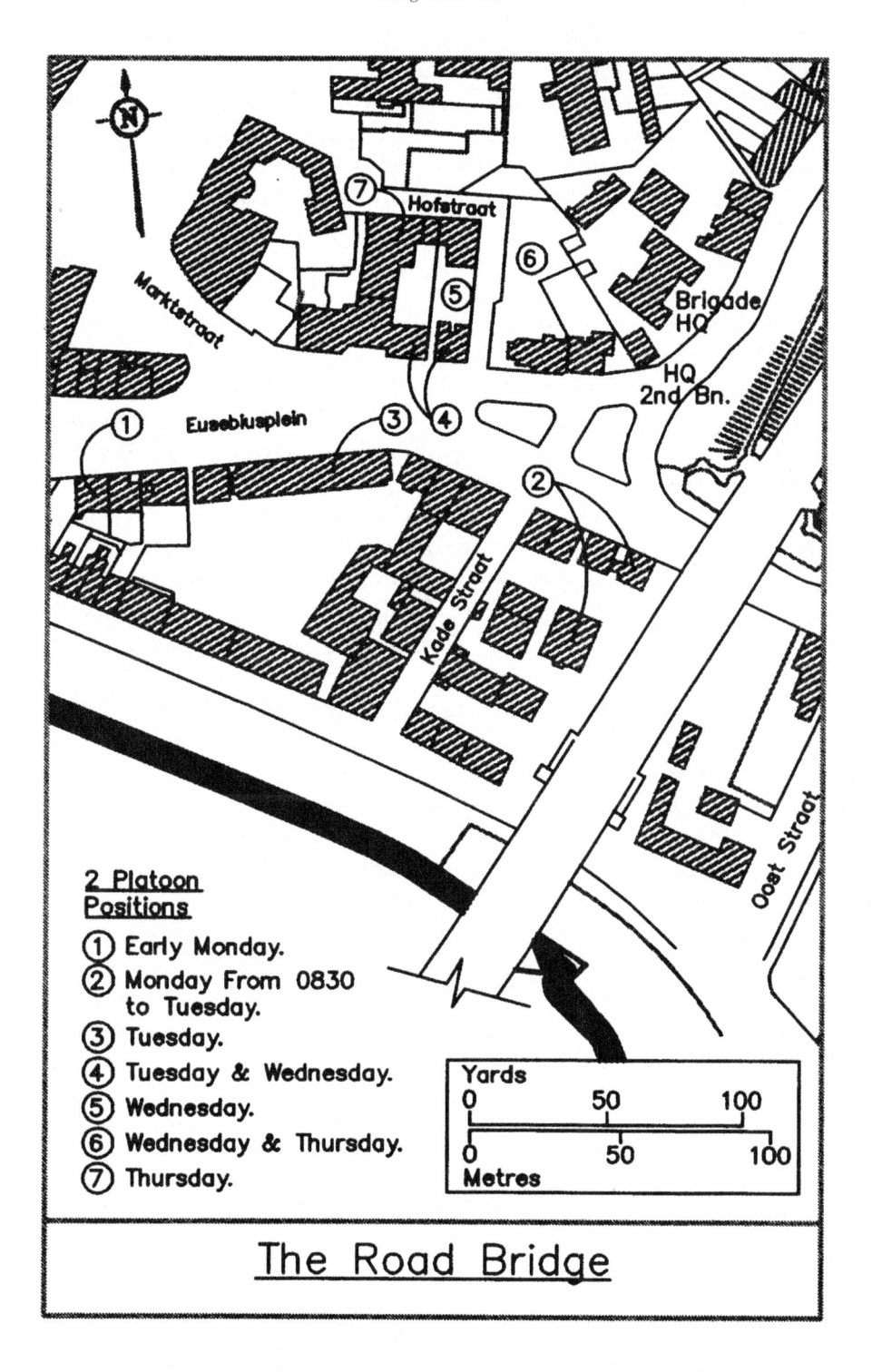

① Early Monday.
② Monday From 0830 to Tuesday.
③ Tuesday.
④ Tuesday & Wednesday.
⑤ Wednesday.
⑥ Wednesday & Thursday.
⑦ Thursday.

The Road Bridge

Company ordered Sapper Carpenter to collect some PIAT bombs and come with him. Tom did so and in the process also collected another PIAT team. Under the ramp for the bridge, from forty feet away, the Captain fired a PIAT and hit one of the tanks. The other crew and Tom fired and it was enough for the tanks to withdraw. The tank that was hit also moved off which didn't surprise Tom. *"We knew we didn't have much chance of knocking them out, but our mates needed help, so we just went out and scared them off."* [65]

When Sapper Carpenter returned Captain O'Callaghan asked, *"Where the hell have you been?"* [66]

By now the houses that No. 2 Platoon was defending had been set on fire so they had to evacuate. The twenty-five men that were left of the platoon made a dash across the Kadestraat without suffering any further casualties. The next building they held was 21 Eusebiusplein and it was still close to the sea of flames that had engulfed the houses by the bridge. Soon, the Germans were using phosphorous shells on this house, trying to burn them out. At which time, Corporal Evans was seriously wounded and Sappers Close, Russell and Rogers were killed. All three men had been fighting at the bridge and all three have no known graves. Their bodies had to be left behind when the house they were in caught fire and was destroyed.[67]

The following three statements are from Captain O'Callaghan in a report he wrote upon his return to England concerning the fate of his men. Regarding Sapper Close, *"He was killed during the shelling of a building occupied by his section. I personally saw his body lying near the debris of the house, and identified it by the unmistakable large amount of fair curly hair, blue eyes, and well built body of this sapper."* [68]

Sappers Russell and Rogers, *"These men did not report after the house they occupied was destroyed. They were in the same room as Sapper Close."* [69]

Corporal Evans, *"This N.C.O. was severely wounded in the house I have mentioned already in the above statements. He was taken to the R.A.P. and I was afterwards told by a medical orderly that he died on the same day. I do not know the name of the orderly and I have not been able to verify this statement since I have been home."* [70]

With the building on fire they had to move again. Under cover of smoke they crossed the Eusebiusplein. Carpenter, *"I was with the first group to go to some houses located at the Marktsraat and about halfway across we caught up on a low slung wire and were thrown back in a heap. With encouragement from O'Callaghan we went out once more, in crouched run and surprisingly made it with no casualties. We took over a house on the corner of Markstraat and the Hofstnaat which still provided us with a good field of fire towards the ramp, but ammunition was now becoming scarce and food and water nonexistent. Our PIAT had been firing its armour piercing rounds, penetrating outer brick walls."* [71]

Inside the house was a bed-ridden old lady and the only thing that the men could do for her was to move her bed away from the window. German tank and self propelled guns were becoming very active, but they were careful to keep well out of range of our anti-tank guns. Captain O'Callaghan, *"88mm shelling direct started at our Anti-Tank guns, but the gunners 'stayed put'. Message from the General telling us to hold on reached the Platoon. Everybody was still quite confident and I considered myself lucky to have such a spirited bunch of men. Our casualties amounted to about a dozen. By now, apart from Sapper John Hogg, they were all wounded and were treated in the Regimental Aid Post. I had good reports from the medics."* [72]

By the end of Tuesday, the Oosterbeek perimeter had been formed and any hope of getting to Colonel Frost's reinforced battalion at the bridge had been lost.

Despite the fact that the Borders to the north of the company's position engaged and disabled two enemy tanks, things were looking pretty bleak as Major Winchester describes, *"The whole of Wednesday was rather unpleasant for us. We were constantly and heavily shelled and mortared, and suffered a steady dribble of casualties from mortar bombs bursting in the trees above us. During the day, the enemy attacked SONNENBERG house nine times. Some of their attacks were ill-prepared and half-hearted and all were beaten off. Towards the evening he attacked heavily with infantry supported by a self-propelled gun and flame-throwing tank. Mines hastily laid across a forest track halted the flame-thrower, and our 17 pounder anti-tank gun "brewed it up". The SP gun then withdrew. By the evening we had repulsed all attacks without many casualties. The latest news was that Second Army patrols were nearing the South bank of the river. Food and ammunition were beginning to run short, but everyone was in good heart. It was only the constant mortaring which worried us, caused continuous casualties, and prevented sleep."* [73]

In the early afternoon Captain Heggie and approximately fifteen men of No. 3 Platoon were sent to defend Heveadorp ferry in a position five hundred yards west of the Borders' position. The infantry in that area were hard-pressed and short of troops. The CRE thought that we should make every effort to hold the ferry as long as possible. Consequently, this party was ordered to sit on the actual ferry while the infantry held the high ground overlooking it.[74]

That evening, Captain Green, Adjutant R.E., was ferried to the south bank of the river at Heveadorp ferry by Captain Heggie's party. He was sent to contact 30 Corps. The 2nd Army was reported to have reached Nijmegen.[75]

Meanwhile at the bridge, the Germans had been attacking all day long and the sappers had lost count of how many times they had opened fire on them. The platoon was now down to fourteen men when the Germans started shelling the house. The elderly lady was killed and her house was rapidly becoming a pile of rubble. Captain O'Callaghan ordered the men to move to the back garden and to dig in. Once there, mortar shells started landing amongst them. Sapper Carpenter, *"At about 1600 hours during heavy shelling and mortaring I heard a shout, 'we're pulling out'. As I moved to respond my body jerked and I went down as though someone had thrown a house brick at my back. With blood gushing over my neck and face I tried again to get up but my limbs would not respond. After a time I was aware of Corporal Lancaster cutting at my uniform and placing a shell dressing. Sergeant 'Sonnie' Gibbons was there giving covering fire. They both helped me to my feet and across into a fruit and vegetable warehouse where the remnants of our depleted force had taken up position. The enemy was following up his attack and grenades followed us into the building."*[76]

Captain O'Callaghan, *"At 2000 hours the house was shelled and the platoon was ordered to cross the Hofstraat into some gardens and join the other forces near the 2nd Battalion Headquarters. The Platoon arrived in the area and as I couldn't find any officers, I ordered the men to dig in, giving cover for the Battalion Headquarters. Lance Corporal W.E. Johnson put up a magnificent show holding off the enemy infantry with a captured machine gun, although he was wounded. It was at that moment that I was hit in the head and neck at about midnight and was 'out' for about thirty minutes."*[77]

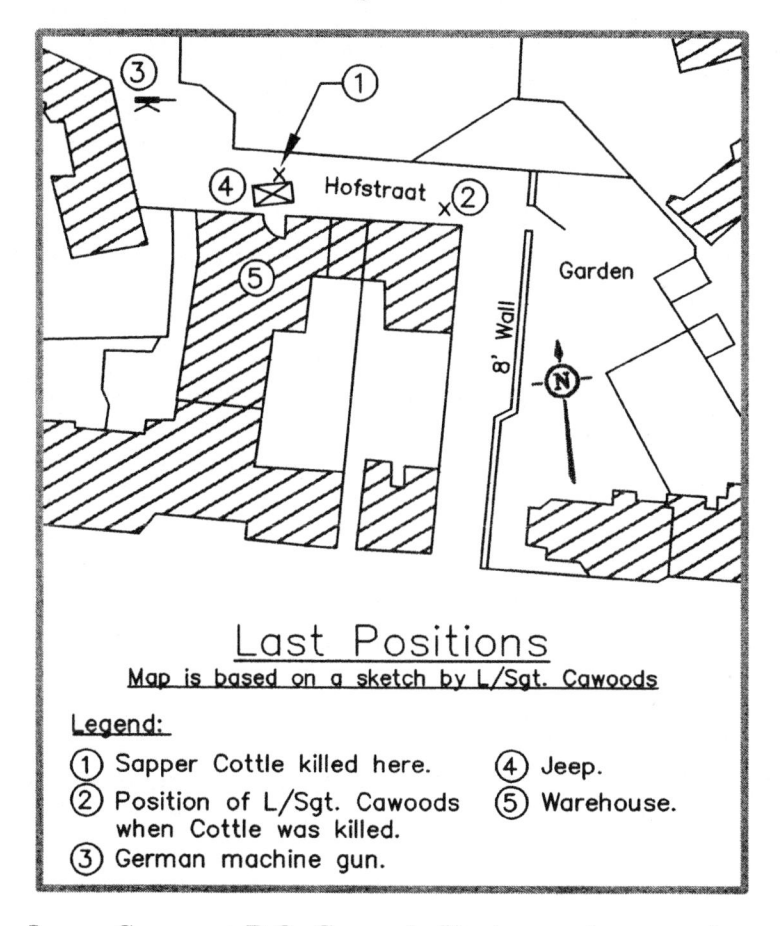

Last Positions
Map is based on a sketch by L/Sgt. Cawoods

Legend:
① Sapper Cottle killed here.
② Position of L/Sgt. Cawoods when Cottle was killed.
③ German machine gun.
④ Jeep.
⑤ Warehouse.

Lance Sergeant R.O. Cawood, *"(we) were down to about ten men and we were in the back gardens of building five, German mortar shells were landing in the garden and causing casualties."* [78]

Captain O'Callaghan, *"I left the rear garden when we got by a jeep. A German soldier called out from a corner 'Englander?' and threw a stick grenade at us. Sapper A.A. Cottle was on my right, and the other Sappers were on my left. As Sapper Cottle went down and was going to fire, the stick greande hit him in the chest and killed him instantly. At this point I was lying flat on the ground."* [79]

L/Sgt Cawoods has a slightly different story. He says that he gave an order for the men to dash up the street (Hofstraat) to gain better cover and that the men left the back garden through a gateway in pairs, and made for a warehouse about halfway up the street on the left. A jeep was stalled slightly diagonally across the street on the left side near the warehouse door. Lance Sergeant Cawood and Sapper Cottle were the last pair to go and Sapper Cottle went first followed by L/Sgt Cawood. Sapper Cottle was hit by German MG34 tracer bullets by the stalled jeep and fell, mortally wounded. Bullets were hitting the ground all around Lance Sergeant Cawood as he ran, but he made it into the warehouse. He never saw the Captain.[80]

While serving with the South Staffords in the eastern sector of the perimeter, what was left of Corporal Pink's reinforced section was manning a house on Benedendorpweg near the old Church. A shell exploded in the house and Sapper W.H. Wilson was wounded in the legs and arms, Sapper Cyril R. Williams was wounded in the foot and Corporal Pink was killed.[81]

Sapper C.R. Williams, *"I was then taken by a jeep to the Regimental Aid Post which was in the house of Kate ter Horst and her family and remained there till the last day."* [82]

The other wounded man was Sapper Bill Wilson, who spoke very highly of Kate ter Horst. *"She was a very nice lady. She used to bring round cherry brandy and advocaat. A Captain Martin was looking after us, but it was a case of just cutting your boots off and patching you up, you were just left there unless you called for help; the orderlies were overwhelmed. Anyone with a really serious wound was in trouble, and many of them died. Others were killed when the German tanks opened fire, the shots going through the building without exploding. We all looked like Red Indians then, covered with brick dust"* [83]

Captain Heggie and his few men remained in position at the ferry until midnight, when they and the infantry were driven back by enemy flame-throwing tanks. Sapper J. Poultney, *"It was my thought that we could have easily ferried a Battalion over the Rhine on the first day. The hours frittered towards when for the first time we heard sounds of the battle, also an engine that had the whine of a tracked vehicle. Now we heard footsteps of someone running in our direction. A man of the Border Regiment came towards us, saying that a self-propelled gun was attacking them. It was dark by this time; the sound of battle jolted us. Two orders were given, the first `Come on, I'll get you out of this' and the second order was that Lance Sergeant Hugh Lake was to stay at the position. The rest left the area by a path to the east that meandered across the flat polder until we came upon a unit of the Artillery. At the time I wasn't very impressed by their armament. We had a discussion, especially as no one was in charge we collectively decided to stay, and then in alongside a dry stonewall of the old church."* [84]

As his men retreated, Lake remained half submerged in the reeds by the water's edge only two or three hundred yards from the enemy. Part of his citation for Distinguished Conduct Medal reads: `*During the night 20th/21st the ferry was heavily attacked and the protective party forced to withdraw. Lance-Sergeant Lake, however, lay up near the ferry on the water edge, half submerged. He loosened the cables and prepared to disable the ferry should the enemy attempt to use it. He remained on his own under fire within 200 yards of the enemy without food or water until the early morning of 22nd September, when he rejoined the unit, wounded and exhausted with detailed information of the enemy's movements and disposition on the river bank.*" [85]

Not all men were about to retreat in time. Corporal L. Ragget, Commander 11 Section, No 3 Platoon, *"...the Germans put in an armoured attack from the high ground of the Westerbouwing, and I was wounded in the leg by a stick grenade. Sapper Charlie Seymour helped me to a Field Dressing Station. From there I was taken to the Tafelberg Hotel. In the next few days I was moved to several first Aid Posts including the St. Elisabeth Hospital."* [86]

Corporal Pink and Sapper Cottle were the only two company men to die on the 20th. However, that being said, Sapper Gilbert Gwilliam was killed near the ferry early on the 21st.[87]

At the bridge around 0100 hours on Thursday, those fit enough to break out were ordered to try to get through the German lines. These were Captain O'Callaghan, Sergeant Gibbons, Corporal Lancaster and a few sappers. Sapper Carpenter was not one of them who wasn't in condition to move. He says that, *"My own condition had deteriorated and I was drifting in and out of consciousness. Four days and nights without sleep, I had lost a lot of blood from the wound to my shoulder and back and the lack of food and water was taking its toll. Events taking place around me were so unreal, remote, like in a dream. I was aware of whistles, explosions and shouts. It was daylight and the Germans were picking up the wounded. I was removed by stretcher first to a local school, then with other wounded, to St. Elisabeth's Hospital, after that I was put on a cattle truck at a railway siding with a lot of other wounded and ended up in the prison camp, after all this time I was finally treated for my wounds. Even now when I pass through one of those security machines at the airport, I trigger off the beeper every time, I just tell them that it is my piece of Arnhem that I carry around."* [88]

Captain O'Callaghan, *"Around 0800 hours Sergeant E. Gibbons, Lance Corporal W.E. Johnson, Driver P.H. Weddell and one man from the 1st Squadron, R.E. were with the wounded. Corporal A.A. Lancaster was still unwounded but a prisoner. During the morning I was taken to the Arnhem Municipal Hospital. Sergeant Gibbons was taken away by ambulance jeep. Sapper H.W. Thomson was also there."* [89]

For No. 2 Platoon the battle at the bridge was over and, for all intensive purposes, the battle at the bridge was more or less over as well. Those who survived and couldn't escape were taken away to a hospital or to a prisoner of war camp.

At 0600 hours mortar fire opened on company position at the Sonnenberg and continued during most of the day. It was more accurate than the previous day's fire and one jeep and trailer was destroyed.

Captain Heggie and approximately eight sappers returned to the company area around 0900 hours.[90] On the morning of the 21st, Sapper Poultney, *"Morning of first light I saw a church beyond a stonewall, so made towards it. It was the old church along the Benedendorpsweg. We hung around believing someone knew we must be in the vicinity. Approximately midmorning, as now word had reached us we decided to make our way towards our initial position. The going was slow due to intermittent mortar fire and shells. Heading along tracks going north, just before reaching the tramway, Captain Heggie appeared. He had been sent down to the ferry but was now on his way back. The mortar fire had reached near crescendo proportions by this time. With the Captain leading we made a desperate race to our original second day slit trenches."* This was along the Utrechtseweg where the monument now stands. *"Sapper Alec Lawson was helping casualties to the First Aid Post that was the first dwelling west on the Utrechtseweg southern side. He appeared to dedicate himself to the task that certainly took some courage. By now our digging had the appearance of miniature World War One trenches, deeper, deeper with every burst of mortar. Steps were cut to both evacuate and to observe. Beginning to feel the stress of the assault, lack of water, food, orders and information, personally I became subject to claustrophobia, being trapped was not for me, never has been. I could not deal with the problem of doing nothing to alter the situation but crouch in the trench. So far no one of my small group had fired a single shot at the enemy and strangely enough, this phenomenon continued to the end. Without* *even caution, with my head and shoulders exposed, I glanced everywhere at everything in sight, but there was nothing but debris. About to drop back when a mortar bomb exploded, I am sure directly in front, a few yards away. I imagined my face squashed, feeling all over my features. No wounds but the most horrible sensation I have ever encountered. We moved to the bushes, I told Sapper Alec Lawson that what I wanted most was water. His reply was, `I have been told there is a pump somewhere over the road perhaps they know where it is'. At that moment we went over the road together. There was a gate and Alec returned to his position. I approached and opened the door to a wide hall running straight through the house. No one was around so I went along the hallway in a direct line out of the backdoor. At this back door I believe there were steps, I glanced left and right and was shocked to see a heap of bodies, for all 1st Airborne men, the degradation was unbearable."* 91

Major Winchester, *"During the morning, we had the cheering news that medium guns from Second Army were firing in support of the Western and Eastern sides of the divisional perimeter. This did not assist us in our sector, but the sound of their heavy shells pounding the enemy was most heartening."* 92

As per usual the enemy continued to shell and mortar the area in support of a few minor attacks. These were repulsed easily. The Germans also produced a loud-speaker and tried to convince the British to surrender by telling them that their position was hopeless. This was greeted with derisive catcalls and very soon their broadcast apparatus was shelled into silence.93

Movement inside the perimeter was risky as Sapper Knight says, *"When I had to collect a message from the HQ I had to dash across the road at the back and head down the stairs that are at the side of the building all the time under sniper fire, a well placed German sniper had infiltrated in the night and had the entrance covered, he was very good and quite a few blokes had been hit. I just put my head down and made a quick dash, if the message wasn't ready we runners would try to get our heads down or maybe get a bite to eat or just be glad to be out of the terrible mortar and shell fire outside, by then it was very heavy. On one occasion there were too many of us crammed into the stairwell and the Officers couldn't get past to do their jobs, so one bright spark ordered out all those not on duty and that included me, so I had to stay outside the window while the messages were passed out to me through a small window at ground level. I had to lay down here in all that bloody shell fire and wait until Colonel*

Myers passed me a message through this little window and then I had to run the gauntlet and deliver it, he would keep saying to me, "are you all right Knight?, are you still there?'. Sometimes I had trouble hearing him because of all the noise outside, and when I mentioned it was a bit dangerous out here he replied, `shut up Knight, stop complaining and wait there, there are people a lot worse off than you' at that moment I couldn't see another soul above ground except me, so I wondered who was worse off and who the hell he was talking about. When nothing was heard from the window for a while I scampered off into a hole with Glider Pilot until things quieted down." [94]

In the late afternoon, Captain Heggie and Captain Wetherill were wounded by mortar fire, leaving Major Winchester and Captain Binyon as the only officers of the 9th remaining. Also wounded during the day were Sergeant Telford, Corporal Raggett and Sappers Dane, Robertson and Pedan. Sapper Thomas O. Morris was killed near the van Dolderon laundry. Also, two No. 18 sets and two jeeps were damaged by mortar fire. News from the CRE was that the Polish Independent Parachute Brigade Group dropped south of the river opposite Oosterbeek towards dusk.

At 2000 hours, a group of sappers from different units - all under the control of Major Winchester - were given an assignment that they could have easily performed on the first couple of days while the ferry was still operational. Reinforcements had landed on a field on the south side of the river and they desperately needed on the north side. Under Lieutenant Storrs from headquarters, Lance Sergeant Green and twelve sappers attempted to establish a ferry across the river with recce boats and trailer rafts. The trailers proved to be too heavy and couldn't float. The assignment was unsuccessful and the men returned to the Sonnenberg.[95]

Major Winchester, *"Friday was a perfectly horrid day. My second in command, Captain Wetherill, and Cart Heggie had both been wounded the previous evening and evacuated to the nearest main dressing station where they were later made prisoners. This left me as the sole officer of 9 Fd Coy, except for Captain Binyon who was with his platoon fighting on the South-East perimeter. 4 Para Sqn had also lost two officers, including Major Perkins wounded and a prisoner. Our positions were mortared and shelled very heavily and continuously all day and we had little with which to hit back. We just had to sit and "take it".* [96]

One person who didn't sit around and just take it was Lance Sergeant Lake as his citation reads, *"During 22nd September the unit was running short of food and water. On his own initiative Lance-Sergeant Lake organized a foraging party and with two sappers carried water through intense mortar fire to the company positions."* [97]

At approximately 1030 hours, the CRE crossed the river by recon boat with G.S.O. to contact 30 Corps. Major Winchester was now acting as CRE in addition to being a sector commander of the perimeter defense.[98] It was reported that 2nd Army had linked up with the Polish Independent Parachute Brigade Group. [99]

Movement inside the perimeter wasn't sensitive to rank as Major Winchester had the same problems as Sapper Knight. *"Although divisional HQ was only about 300 yards from my sector HQ it was quite an adventure to get from one place to the other. I had to move from one HQ to the other a number of times during the day and each journey necessitated crossing two roads which were swept by enemy MG fire and evading enemy snipers, who covered the entrance to the cellar in which divisional HQ was established. By this time, all our jeeps had been burnt out by shell and mortar fire and the roads were strewn with debris and fallen branches. I therefore had to do a smart sprint over the distance each time."* [100]

During one of his visits to divisional HQ, he organized a party to ferry more Poles across to the North bank of the river the following evening. [101]

The 22nd was the first and only day of the operation where the 9th didn't lose a man, but sappers Beech, Congreve, Kenny, Martin and Beardall were wounded.[102]

Right: A pre-war postcard showing the Heveadorp ferry, looking north across the river at the Westerbouwing heights. Note the barge tied up on the north shore.
(Geert Maassen)

A Long Tradition

Above: A prewar postcard showing the Heveadorp ferry from the north bank. (Geert Maassen)

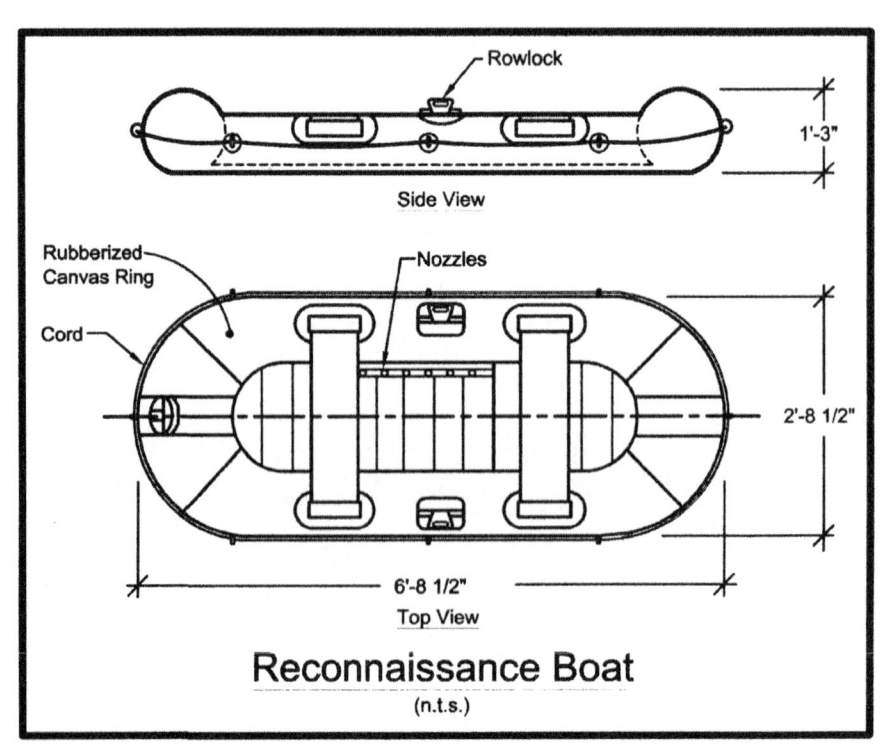

Reconnaissance Boat
(n.t.s.)

Sapper Task

During the D-day drop, the 6th Airborne Division's Field Park Company brought twelve assault boats and forty-eight reconnaissance boats in by glider and were useful. The decision not to bring in all of the 261st Field Park Company and its equipment was to prove costly to the 1st Airborne Division at Arnhem. Twelve assault boats and forty-eight reconnaissance boats would have been very useful in getting the Polish brigade across the river. Their three fresh infantry battalions, plus their support arms, would have been very valuable reinforcements. For a division that was running out of men and ammunition, reinforcements were vital and the plan was to get as many of them across the river as possible.

A platoon commander of the 4th Parachute Squadron, RE, Captain H.F. Brown, *"We reached the river at **698769**, where the banks proved to be firm mud with stone groynes built out into the stream at about 100 yard intervals. Our plan was to attach signal cable fore and aft of the recce boats, and pull them across with two Polish paratroopers in each, then pull them back empty. The river was so wide and fast that the signal cable broke, and we had to resort to rowing one Pole across at a time. Two boats were punctured in reducing the total number to four recce boats and one RAF dinghy. Before the sappers started, they were all almost asleep on their feet and very hungry. One or two automatic weapons were firing just over our heads and an odd mortar bomb disturbed the otherwise swift, unruffled river."* [103]

Lance-Sergeant Lake's presence was certainly felt as his citation records, *"On the evening of 22nd September, less than ten hours after his return, Lance-Sergeant Lake volunteered to accompany a party which was to ferry the Poles across the river Neder Rijn. His knowledge of the river bank materially assisted the ferrying operations. During the return journey Lance-Sergeant Lake was again wounded – this time in the neck."* [104]

By daylight only 52 men had been ferried across. Major Winchester, *"After a beastly wet night spent in trying to ferry some more of the Poles to our side of the river, I returned to the Company HQ in the early hours of the morning. I snatched a few hours of sleep in a very wet slit trench and then found it a pleasure to walk round our defense positions. This necessitated quite a few sprints from one party's position to the next, and did at least get my blood circulation going again."* [105]

Siege Part II

From this point on the story of the 9th is similar to that of the 1st and 4th Parachute Squadrons, R.E. at the Sonnenberg, with all units under heavy mortar fire all day and anxious about the general lack of news as to what was happening on the South bank. On this day, both Lance-Sergeant James Ryder and Sapper John Kelly died of their wounds and were buried in the garden of the Ter Horst family home.

Major Winchester, *"During the day, we had little fresh news of the progress of Second Army. There were intermittent enemy attacks on our sector but none were very serious efforts. We continued to have to "take" the enemy's mortar and shell fire without any means of replying to it. The sappers settled down to holding the position with the minimum of effort and movement, and conserved their energies for the ferrying some of them would again have to do that night."* [106]

At 0023 hours on the 24th, fourteen assault boats finally arrived on the south bank. At 0300 hours a bombardment signalled the start of the 2nd Polish crossing. In charge of the boats were the engineers of the Polish Brigade, while Major Winchester and his sappers helped from the north shore. The operation got one hundred and fifty-three Polish paratroopers across the river.

Back at the Sonnenberg, it was business as usual. Major Winchester, *"By Sunday, food was getting really short. A week earlier we had landed with rations for 48 hours and the expectation of being relieved within three days. During the week we had existed on fruit and vegetables from local gardens and various supplies found in the cellars of private houses. We had also removed the rations from any of our own dead. Now it became increasingly difficult to satisfy our hunger and there is no doubt that hunger made the men weak and less energetic."* [107]

Men tried to find food anywhere they could and it backfired at times. According to Sapper Foster, who was in the next trench over, Lance Sergeant Dodger Green brewed up some soup using 808 plastic explosive to make a fire. Some of the explosives dropped into the soup making all of those who drank it, including Lance Sergeant Green, very ill. [108]

Major Winchester, *"Fortunately, from now on all the men were called upon to do was to stick it out and hold on until the relieving forces reached us. This was none too easy, as casualties were continuous and our men were very thin on the ground. At one time during this day the sole divisional reserve of troops was*

A Long Tradition

eleven sappers under my PT sergeant. This reserve was duly committed on the South-Eastern sector of the perimeter and fought most gallantly until the end." [109]

Corporal W.C.E. Barber, *"During midday I was with the PTI, Sergeant Snow, digging a trench just outside the Old Church when the padre asked if Snow could help him bury some soldiers. Snow asked me if I could find a door to cover the trench we were digging. I ran across the street and found some houses which were heavily damaged. After a while I found one, which was big enough for the trench, but I could not get this door out of its position. At the end I got it loose and was trying to get to our trench. At that moment the Germans began with another mortar attack. I protected myself with the door against the mortar shrapnel. When I arrived at the trench I saw Snow's body lying not far from our trench, headless."* [110]

Upon his return to the company from visiting headquarters, Major Winchester found that Captain Binyon was missing. The Captain's arrival was just before the enemy had attacked with two tanks. Major Winchester, *"He had helped to bombard the enemy tanks with a PIAT and was last seen carrying the PIAT with its last few remaining rounds in an effort to get a flank shot at the tank. He disappeared from view behind some trees within 15 yards of the tank and was not seen again."* [111]

Sapper Alex Lawson was the third man to be killed on the 24th and by the sounds of the performance of the medical orderly, it could have been more. Driver George Fairs' citation for Military Medal reads, *"During the period of 19th-24th 1944 when the company was holding part of the perimeter defences of Oosterbeek the position was continually under mortar fire and men were continually being wounded. Driver Fairs rendered first aid to every casualty immediately when they occurred. He never hesitated to run to the aid of a man whatever the danger from mortar bombs or small arms fire. On the 24th September he was wounded by a splinter but carried on for some time, rendering first aid until he himself was evacuated to hospital. By his complete disregard for his personal safety he showed a magnificent example of fearlessness to his comrades and his immediate first aid to the wounded under fire certainly saved at least three lives."* [112]

Sapper Shepard, *"Defense was our main job and for the rest of the operation I dug a lot of trenches around divisional headquarters. Every trench getting dug pushed us nearer to the hotel, nearly finishing up on the steps. From there I evacuated across the river okay and didn't meet up with any of the 9ᵗʰ until I got to Nijmegen."* [113]

Approximately at 0130 hours on Monday 25ᵗʰ there were reports of Dorsets of the 43 Infantry Division had carried out an assault crossing and attacked the heights opposite the Heveadorp ferry. It was falsely believed that they captured the hill. Around 6.30 am, just after first light, the CRE returned to Divisional Headquarters from the south bank after an adventurous trip to HQ 30 Corps on the South bank of the river. He brought with him the plans for the withdrawal of the division across the river, which 43 Division had then reached with their forward battalions.[114]

Major Winchester, *"Monday 25 September started the same as the previous three days. We expected to have to continue the defence as usual. No one had really considered the possibility of our having to withdraw. The men were hungry and anxious for news; ammunition was very short, but we were in a strong position, had successfully dealt with the enemy's attacks for the past week and, although we were now fewer in numbers, no one doubted that we could continue to hold our positions for a bit longer. In some sectors, however, casualties had been heavy, there were too few troops and the enemy was beginning to establish pockets inside the divisional perimeter."* [115]

Sapper A.T. Williams, *"During this morning I was searching for food and water just outside the old church when I found a jeep, maybe a medical jeep, smashed up by shelling. In the jeep I found a tin of rice pudding and set of clean underwear. I took the rice pudding and the underwear with me in a shelled house. I found a spot under the stairs where I could wash myself. I took off the dirty clothes and had a quick wash and shave and put on the clean underwear. I felt like a new man. I think I was the cleanest man in the area."* [116]

Above: a modern shot of the river and the evacuation site taken from the new café on the Westerbouwing heights. (taken by Author)

Withdrawal

At 1100 hours on the 25th, Major Winchester heard the General's orders for the plan for the withdrawal. Major Winchester, *"It was very simple. The division was to pull out that night along two routes to the river bank, where boats manned by 43 Division and Canadian engineers would ferry us over. Officers were to be told of the withdrawal at 2 pm and the men at 4 pm. Ferrying was to start at 10 pm and continue until all men had been got across the river. Our withdrawal was to be supported by all the artillery fire that 30 Corps could bring to bear. After the General had given out his orders I sprinted back to my sector HQ for the last time."* [117]

Two hours later, he briefed all the officers under his command, Captain George, Captain Cormie and Lieutenant Thomas, as to the method of withdrawal and the route to be taken. The password was *John Bull* and the code word for withdrawal operation was *Berlin.* Then, in the cellar of a small lodge at the entrance to the grounds of Sonnenberg house the Major arranged with the quartermaster for all the men to pool what rations were left and have a final "brew up" at about 1600 hours. [118]

Major Winchester, *"They left their positions in parties of six to eight and, while they ate, I briefed each party about the withdrawal-the reasons for it, the routes to take, where opposition was likely to be met, and many other important details. I had been ordered to lay white tapes along one of the routes of withdrawal personally, as I knew my way about the divisional area fairly well. I had made several trips from the Northern edge of the perimeter by night down to the river, while most of the other troops had remained throughout the defence in one small area. In order to carry out this task I had to hand over the command of my sector to Captain George and gave him the timings according to which each unit had to withdraw."* [119]

At 1600 hours all ranks of 9 Field Company were briefed for withdrawal. Lance Corporal Basil Burton, *"...we were ordered to prepare for withdraw at that night, including binding of our boots with torn strips of blanket to muffle sounds of movement and destruction of supplies to prevent them falling into enemy hands."* [120]

The Company was put under command of Captain George of the 1st Parachute Squadron for withdrawal and at 1940 hours, Major Winchester and four sappers left with many rolls of tracing to tape along the westerly route of withdrawal from near divisional HQ down to the ferrying sites. They had about a mile of tape to lay and it was 2100 hours before they reached the river. Major Winchester, *"We hurried as much as possible, but the need for silence was great-the enemy in places were within 40 yards and we knew many men would soon be following in our tracks- and twice we were interrupted, by local battles. Shortly after we reached the river, the first parties of men began to arrive. Having arrived at the river bank among the first, I undertook the duties of beachmaster. This involved calling forward parties for embarkation as each ferry craft came in, seeing that the wounded were evacuated first and marshalling the troops who were waiting to embark under cover. It was a very dark and rainy night, which was fortunate in most ways, but made control of the embarkation difficult. For a short time, the ferrying went with a swing; then, possibly thinking that we were reinforcing our perimeter rather than evacuating it, the enemy began to shell and mortar the ferrying sites unmercifully. Many of the ferry craft were sunk and casualties on the river bank began to mount. The 43 Divisional sappers, however, kept at it most gallantly and the ferrying proceeded until the early hours of Tuesday morning when daylight prevented any further operations. The discipline on the river bank was excellent. There were very few ferry craft and most of the men had to wait a long time huddled against the river bank under heavy shell and mortar fire. Those who were strong swimmers took to the water, stripped except for their personal weapons, and made room in the boats for non-swimmers and the wounded, of which there were many. The men had made their way to the river in parties of twelve to fourteen (boat loads) and they were embarked as far as possible by units in the order in which they arrived."* [121]

At 2115 hours the first of the troops started to withdraw through company positions and at 2127 hours the company started to withdraw in parties of approximately fifteen, each under a sergeant or senior N.C.O. They moved in single file south towards the river, each man holding firmly onto the tail of the man ahead, with strict orders for absolute silence and security.[122]

Lance Corporal Burton, *"During this time the enemy must have grown suspicious and it's possible that they guessed what was in hand, for the woods between the river and the hotel which we were traversing on our way to the river were heavily strafed by mortar and incandescent phosphorous bombs and we observed several infantry patrols which we successfully evaded. About halfway to the river during particularly heavy mortaring which coin-*

cided with the sighting of a nearby enemy patrol, I was separated from the man ahead of me and was unable to regain contact and so decided to lead my remnant along the general line of evacuation successfully reaching the north bank of the Rhine some time later." [123]

At 2230 hours the first parties of the company reached the river bank south of the church and prepared to cross the river in boats manned by the members of the 23rd Field Company, Royal Canadian Engineers. During the walk down Lance-Sergeant Lake was again wounded, this time badly in the shoulder and back. Fortunately, he and his party made it to the boats where his men carried him aboard.[124]

Sapper Donald A. Wann, *"Instead of shouting and pushing, the troops were marvelous. They waited in a queue, 'like queuing for the pictures' – for about three hours in pouring rain and bitter cold."* [125]

The Sappers of the 43rd Infantry division were under the command of the Divisional CRE Lieutenant-Colonel Henniker who, until a few month's previously, was the CRE of the airborne division. Upon arrival on the south bank, Burton's boat was hailed by Henniker, asking if there were any Sappers aboard. Burton identified himself and was recognized and welcomed by the Lieutenant Colonel who wrote in his memoir, *"I met many old friends: General Urquhart, Eddie Myers and many Sappers tramped past in the dark."* [126]

On the way, two men lost their way and their lives. Sapper Milne wrote this regarding Sappers May and Clarke, *"All I can say is that they were with me until the second last day I was taken prisoner. I was captured on the 26th day of September 1944. The above left me on the 25th September. For eight days the three of us lived in slit trenches. We had to make a retreat from Arnhem and finally landed in a village called Oosterbeek. It was a miracle that none of us were wounded, but up until the last day I saw them, none of us had a scratch. We discussed amongst ourselves, the possibility of us reaching the Rhine and seeing it but in the circumstance I considered it hopeless. May and Clarke thought otherwise. On the eighth day they came over to my slit trench and asked if I was coming with them and try and get across the water but I refused to go and I pleaded with them to stay as I knew they would never stand a chance. That was the last I saw of them. That was at Oosterbeek on 25th September 1944."* He described Clarke as about 5'-9", slim build, wavy hair and was the Dispatch Rider in the company. May was about 5'-8" and was plumper than Clarke.[127]

Major Winchester, *"By about 1 am, men waiting to cross were lying under cover along a long stretch of the river and the ferry boats were beaching at irregular intervals along the whole of this stretch. By this time, I was thoroughly exhausted and my job of beach master was superfluous. The ferry boats were loading whichever party happened to be nearest to them when they beached. I had checked most of my sappers across the river so decided to join them, when a boat beached right opposite me and there was a place to spare. As our boat bumped the South bank I was assisted ashore, scrambled up the flood bank along a white*

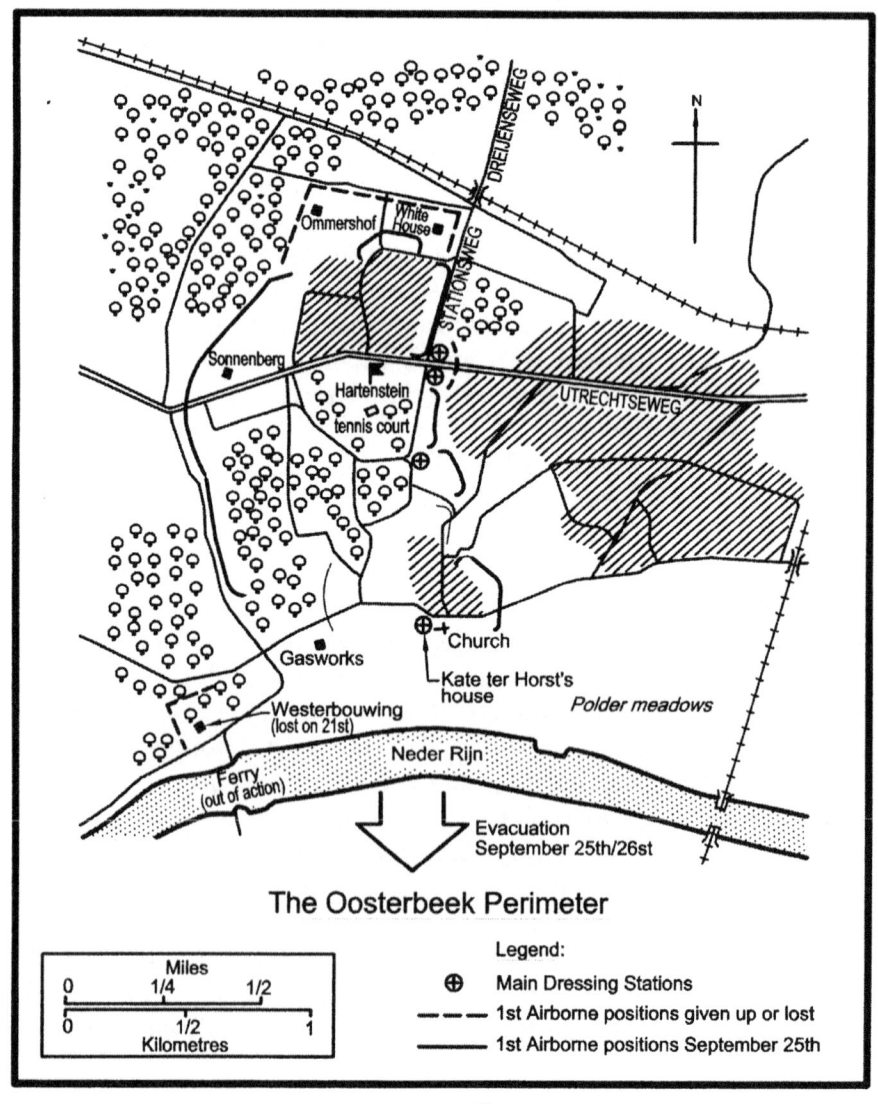

The Oosterbeek Perimeter

Legend:
⊕ Main Dressing Stations
- - - - 1st Airborne positions given up or lost
——— 1st Airborne positions September 25th

tape, and found myself in an apple orchard. After the past nine days of waiting for relief by our own troops it was a great joy to have joined them at last. After a few moments rest, I walked a very very long three miles to DRIEL, where the most delightful cup of tea and rum was given to me in a barn by a unit of 43 Division. Then I collected a couple of blankets, found a lorry bound for NIJMEGEN, jumped in and immediately fell asleep." [128]

Around 0100 hours on the 26th the last element of the company reached the river bank in safety and ferried across the River Rhine. Individuals of the company marched about two and half miles to the Dorsets in Driel, where first aid was rendered and blankets and tea issued. During the remainder of the night, individuals proceeded independently via Valburg to a barracks in Nijmegen, where they were met by 1st Seaborne Lift and fed and accommodated for the next day. Most of the company slept and rested all day until the late afternoon, when it moved to another barracks in Nijmegen.[129]

Unfortunately, not all men made it across. Many were wounded and weren't capable of making the journey while others were simply out of the loop. Corporal W.C.E. Barber, *"The whole company seemed to be split up towards the end of the battle; I was dug in outside the Pietersberg for a while and then went to the Old Church, I never received any message about the withdrawal and was taken prisoner the next day, along with some other Sappers after everyone had gone."* [130]

Corporal Raggett was one of the wounded and was taken prisoner in the morning at the end of Pietersbergsweg. He was taken to Apeldoorn before being put on a cattle wagon and was transported to a hospital in Germany. *"When I arrived at the hospital I found out that the Senior British Officer was Australian from the Medical Corps. He later gave me a skin graft on my left leg. By Christmas that year, I was due to be transported to a Prisoner of War camp, Stalag IXC. But I managed to avoid going for about four weeks, but after those four weeks I had to go. Because there was little or no transport we had to march a few miles from the hospital to Stalag IXC in the north. The march played havoc with my wound and also my left ankle and leg were very swollen. When I arrived in the camp the food was very scarce, the daily ration was a plate of sauerkraut and a slice of German black bread. Fortunately, we had the Red Cross parcels, which kept us going. The Americans liberated the camp in April 1945."* [131]

After Arnhem

On 27 September those of the 9th who had successfully made it across the river received a new issue of clothing and equipment as they recovered in Nijmegen. Around 1130 hours on 28 September the company moved by motor transport from Nijmegen to an airfield near Brussels where they flew back home. Major Winchester, *"It was good to be back again, but a roll call of the company the next day was a very saddening proceeding. Out of 8 officers and over 200 sappers who had left ENGLAND by air a fortnight before, all that answered their names were myself and 56 sappers."* [132]

During the process of rebuilding the company Major Winchester wanted 'jumpers', as the move was to make the company parachutists as well as glider men. This might have been a result of the new 'Airborne Squadron, RE' War Establishment that became effective in March 1945. The reorganization was in reaction to the report 'Lessons Learned At Arnhem', which stated that a restructuring of the company and its resources was needed.

In late February the unit took part in 'Exercise Amber'. This was in preparation for a drop in the Hamburg area towards the end of the war. Rumours of them being sent to the Far East to fight Japan began to circulate. These ended in April when they started to prepare to go to Norway. In May 1945, the 9th went with the division into Norway to disarm the Germans stationed there. It was there that they finally learned what happened to the ill-fated 'Operation Freshman'. The men who had survived the glider crashes were executed as spies and saboteurs.

In July, an advance party of the 9th was sent to India in preparation for a move there. Fortunately, the war ended there before the company could get involved. Over the next years, like the company had been since its beginning, they were sent to wherever they were needed. Service in Palestine was next followed by being part of the British Army Of The Rhine in 1948, England in 1950, Cyprus and Egypt in 1952, Cyprus in 1956, Suez in 1956, Cyprus and Jordon in 1957, Falkland Islands in 1982 and Rwanda in 1994 to name a few places during their long journey.[133]

In addition to a long tradition of travelling the world, the unit's name had been changed numerous times. It is now known as the 9th Parachute Squadron Royal Engineers.

After Word

Since their birth in 1787, the 9th have more or less been in every major action that the British Empire has seen and the battle of Arnhem was no exception. Members of the company fought from the landing zone to the Arnhem Road Bridge, with actions at the ferry, the Wolfhezen Hotel, the railway bridge, the pontoon bridge, the museum, the Sonnenberg and at the eastern sector of the perimeter with Lonsdale Force. And they paid the price for it. Of all the units with twenty men or more, the 9th had the highest death rate of 22.7%*. Granted that almost half of this number were killed when one of their gliders crashed, but the remaining figures are still high and they show how involved in the fighting the company was.

Much has been written about the poor planning of the operation at the higher levels and one example pertaining to the Royal Engineers is the fact that skilled tradesman of the engineering units were 'wasted' fighting as infantry. Yet, mistakes were made at the lower levels as well. The large number of bicycles that had been brought by the company were of little use and took too much space in the gliders, where more personnel or other equipment such as heavier weapons or boats could have been brought instead. The boats would have been invaluable in getting one of Colonel Frost's companies across the river to attack the south end of the bridge on the first day. They certainly would have gotten the Poles across the river in greater numbers.

Even the Heveadorp ferry would have served in this purpose, but at the start of the operation everyone was focused too much on the bridges. It was this tunnel-vision like obsession with the bridges that was the downfall of many, including No. 2 Platoon. Captain O'Callaghan and his platoon should never have gone to the road bridge, but I do not blame him. He had been infected with the *'get to the bridge disease'* that had been postulated by the General staff. Instead, the platoon would have been more valuable under the control of the CRE. Whatever task they were given would have been better than being wiped out at the bridge.

Since the beginning of warfare, engineers have been finding ways of transporting armies across rivers and at least some of the engineers at Arnhem should have been concentrating on this task from the very beginning. Instead, by the time they were given a sapper task to do, the lack of food, sleep and proper equipment hindered their ability to improvise a means of crossing the river. The rafts that were made from trailers were too heavy to even float by themselves and the wire that they tried to use to pull the recon boats across was far too thin. Was there another way? I think yes. A platoon of engineers of the U.S. 101st Airborne Division at Zon improvised a footbridge and then rafts after the bridge there was blown. The platoon was given only one job to concentrate on** and that allowed them to find a way across the canal by finding stockpiles of lumber and steel drums.

On the first day, No. 2 Platoon at Arnhem was given the task of capturing a bridge and that was the genesis of their problems. Likewise, from the first day Nos. 1 and 3 Platoons were also given an infantry task that they shouldn't have been given. So once again, like so many times in their history, the company at Arnhem was a victim of not being allowed to perform the tasks that they were designed to do. It was another example in their long tradition of being misused.

*These are based on figures supplied by Martin Middlebrook's book, `Arnhem' who has the 9th with 194 men going to Arnhem, with 44 KIA, 71 evacuated and 79 missing. These numbers are not totally accurate. Patrick Pronk in `Airborne Engineers' had 220 men going in, with 43 KIA, 1 officer and 56ish men being evacuated and the rest becoming POWs. Major Winchester is quoted saying that of the over 200 men that went to Arnhem, only he and 56 sappers came back.
** Later on they also fought as infantry in defense of the bridge. See MGES #5 `Bridging Hell's Highway'

End Notes:

A Brief History:
1 'The 9th 1787-1960: The History of The British Army's Only Remaining Parachute Engineer Unit' by Tom Purves
2 p146 'An Image At War' by Mark Henniker
3 'The 9th 1787-1960: The History of The British Army's Only Remaining Parachute Engineer Unit' by Tom Purves

Operation Market Garden:
4 'British Amry Of World War Two War Establishment Tables: Northwest Europe June 1944-May 1945 Volume VIII The Airborne Divisions Part I' by Gary Kennedy
5 'Winchester
6 'CRE 1 Airborne Div Op Instruction No. 1: Provisional Notes on CRE's Verbal Orders'
7 'CRE 1 Airborne Div Op Instruction No. 1: Provisional Notes on CRE's Verbal Orders'
8 Acccount: Tom Carpenter
9 p97 'We Fought At Arnhem'
10 'Then And Now'
11 Account: Tom Carpenter
12 'The 9th 1787-1960: The History of The British Army's Only Remaining Parachute Engineer Unit' by Tom Purves
13 'The 9th 1787-1960: The History of The British Army's Only Remaining Parachute Engineer Unit' by Tom Purves
14 'The 9th 1787-1960: The History of The British Army's Only Remaining Parachute Engineer Unit' by Tom Purves
15 p81 'Arnhem: The Airborne Battle' by Martin Middleton
16 'Airborne Engineers The Shiny 9th: An Illustrated History of the 9th (Airborne) Field Company Royal Engineers 1939-1945' by Patrick Pronk
17 Then And Now
18 War Diary / Account: Jardine
19 Account: Tom Carpenter
20 'The 9th 1787-1960: The History of The British Army's Only Remaining Parachute Engineer Unit' by Tom Purves
21 Account: A.T. Williams
22 Winchester / War Diary
23 Account: Foster
24 pp113-114 'We Fought At Arnhem'
25 Winchester / Account Shepard
26 p41 Remember Arnhem
27 War Diary / 'Arnhem' Middlebrook
28 pp117-119 'Arnhem' by Middlebrook
29 Account: A.T. Williams
30 Account: Winchester / War Diary
31 Account: Thorne / Roll Of Honour / War Diary
32 War Diary
33 Account: Captain O'Callaghan
34 p110 'We Fought At Arnhem'
35 Account: Captain O'Callaghan
36 'The 9th 1787-1960: The History of The British Army's Only Remaining Parachute Engineer Unit' by Tom Purves
37 Report: 'Lessons From Arnhem'

38	p121 'We Fought At Arnhem'
39	'B Company Arrived'
40	'Airborne Engineers: The Shiny 9th' / 'We Fought At Arnhem' / 'Engineers At The Bridge'
41	Account: Winchester
	Monday 18 September:
42	'We Fought At Arnhem'
43	p218 'A Drop Too Many'
44	Account: O'Callaghan
45	Account: O'Callaghan
46	War Diary / p159 'We Fought At Arnhem'
47	Report: Thompson
48	Account: Winchester
49	War Diary
50	p59 'Airborne Engineers'
51	War Diary
52	Interview: Knight
53	Interview: Knight
54	War Dairy / p52 'Gunners At Arnhem'
55	Account: Winchester
56	Account: Perkins
57	War Diary
58	Account: Winchester
59	Account: Johnston
60	War Dairy
61	Account: Winchester
62	War Diary
63	Account: Winchester / War Diary
64	Account: Winchester
65	Letter to Barry Dougherty
66	p301 'Arnhem' Middlebrook
67	War Diary
68	Report: O'Callaghan
69	Report: O'Callaghan
70	Report: O'Callaghan
71	Account: Carpenter
72	Account: O'Callaghan
73	Account: Winchester
74	Account: Winchester / War Diary
75	War Diary
76	Account: Carpenter
77	Account: O'Callaghan
78	Account: Cawood
79	Account: O'Callaghan
80	Account: Cawood
81	War Diary
82	p66 'Airborne Engineers'
83	p379 'Arnhem' Middlebrook
84	Account: Poultry
85	Citation: Lake
86	Account: Ragget
87	Roll Of Honour

88   Account: Carpenter
89   Account: O'Callaghan
90   `Arnhem' Middlebrook / War Diary
91   Account: Poultry
92   Account: Winchester
93   Account: Winchester
94   Interview: Knight
95   War Diary
96   Account: Winchester
97   Citation: Lake
98   Account: Winchester
99   War Diary
100 Account: Winchester
101 Account: Winchester
102 War Diary

Sapper Task:

103 Account: O'Callaghan
104 Citation: Lake
105 Account: Winchester

Siege Part II:

106 Account: Winchester
107 Account: Winchester
108 Account: Foster
109 Account: Winchester
110 Account: Barber
111 Account: Winchester
112 Citation: Fairs / Roll Of Honour
113 Account: Shepard
114 War Dairy / Account: Winchester
115 Account: Winchester
116 Account: A.T. Williams

Withdrawal

117 Account: Winchester
118 War Diary / Account: Winchester
119 Account: Winchester
120 War Diary / Burton
121 Account: Winchester
122 War Diary
123 Account: Burton
124 Citation: Lake
125 Account: Wann
126 Account: Burton / `An Image Of War'
127 Account: Milne
128 Account: Winchester
129 War Diary
130 Account: Barber
131 Account: Raggett

After Arnhem

132 War Diary / Account: Winchester
133 `The 9th 1787-1960: The History of The British Army's Only Remaining Parachute Engineer Unit' by Tom Purves

GVI RI

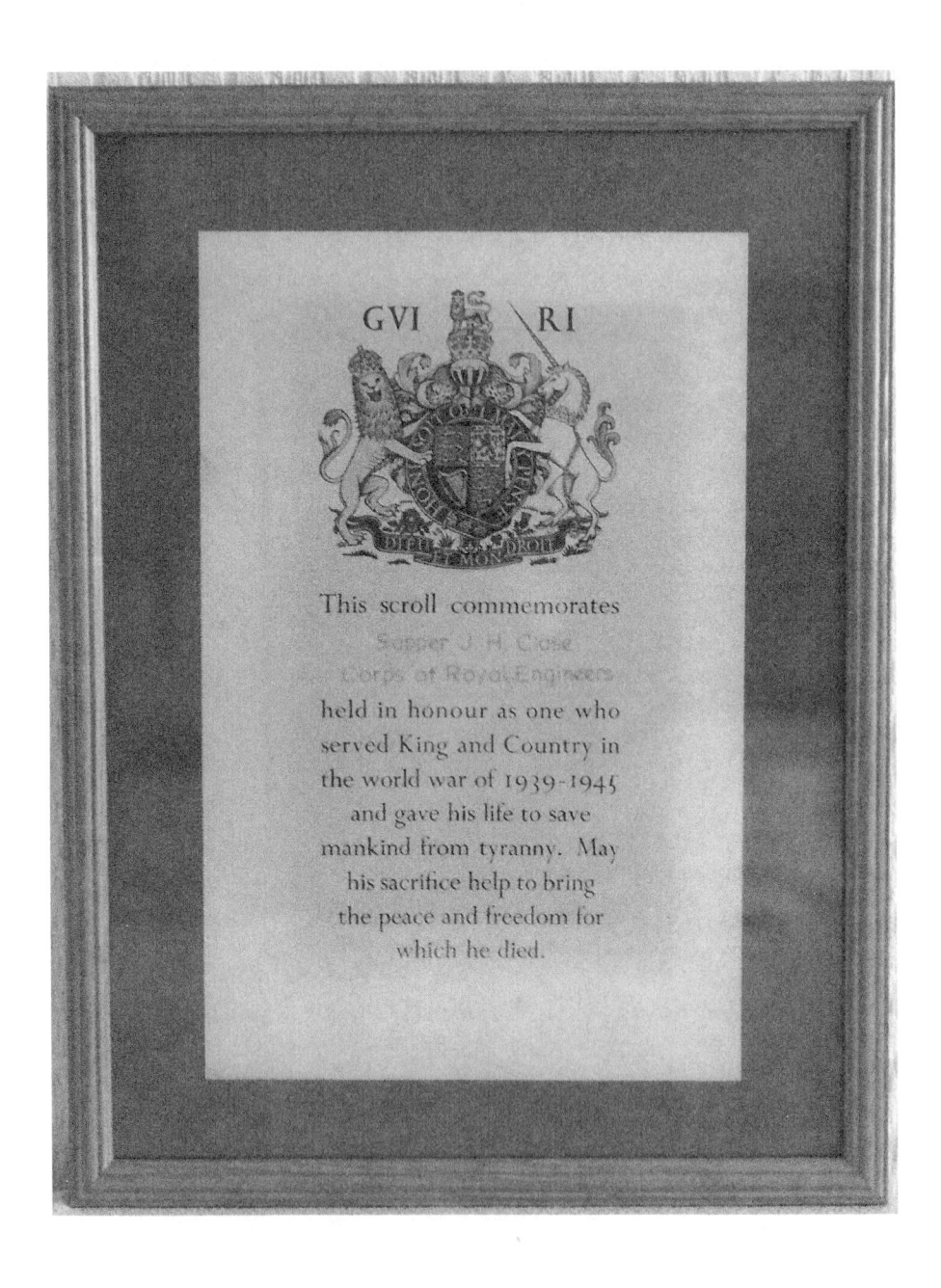

This scroll commemorates
Sapper J. H. Close
Corps of Royal Engineers
held in honour as one who
served King and Country in
the world war of 1939-1945
and gave his life to save
mankind from tyranny. May
his sacrifice help to bring
the peace and freedom for
which he died.

Roll Of Honour

Allen, Roy H. L/Sgt.;
Age 31. Killed when his glider broke apart on September 17th 1944.

Beale, Joseph C. Spr;
Age 18. Killed when his glider broke apart on September 17th 1944.

Burrows, William H. L/Cpl.;
Age 29. Killed when his glider broke apart on September 17th 1944.

Calvert, Cyril W, Spr.;
Age 25. Killed when his glider broke apart on September 17th 1944.

Carney, Robert, Spr.;
Age 23. Killed when his glider broke apart on September 17th 1944.

Clampitt, Arthur L, Cpl.;
Age 24. Killed when his glider broke apart on September 17th 1944.

Cuthbertson, Arthur, Spr.;
Age 24. Killed when his glider broke apart on September 17th 1944.

Davis, Frederick, A.S., Spr.;
Age 26. Killed when his glider broke apart on September 17th 1944.

Evans, John, Spr.;
Age 25. Killed when his glider broke apart on September 17th 1944.

Fernyhough, John, Spr.;
Age 24. Killed when his glider broke apart on September 17th 1944.

Godfrey, Edward J.;
Age 25. Killed when his glider broke apart on September 17th 1944.

Hall, Arthur, Spr.;
Age unknown. Killed when his glider broke apart on September 17th 1944.

Holtham, Douglas, E, Spr.;
Age 25. Killed when his glider broke apart on September 17th 1944.

Oakey, Arthur F., Sgt.;
Age 30. Killed when his glider broke apart on September 17th 1944.

Pickburn, Edward V. L/Cpl.;
Age 27. Killed when his glider broke apart on September 17th 1944.

Sheppard, Edward E. Spr.;
Age 21. Killed when his glider broke apart on September 17th 1944.

Street, Arthur, R. Spr.;
Age 22. Killed when his glider broke apart on September 17th 1944.

Turner, Cyril, Spr.;
Age 27. Killed when his glider broke apart on September 17th 1944.

Watt, Arthur G. Spr.;
Age 26. Killed when his glider broke apart on September 17th 1944.

Westfield, Jack Spr.;
Age 32. Killed when his glider broke apart on September 17th 1944.

Williamson, John Spr.;
Age 25. Killed when his glider broke apart on September 17th 1944.

Holdstock, Raymond F, Spr.;
Age 30. Was killed on landing on September 17th 1944.

Timmins, Roy E.J. Lt.;
Age 23. Was killed near the Wolfhezen Hotel on September 17th 1944.

Greig, Peter, Spr.;
Age 41. Died of wounds on September 18th 1944.

Russell, Ronald V. Spr.;
Age 24. Was killed on September 18th 1944. No known grave.

Takle, William T.N., L/Cpl.;
Age 27. Was killed on September 18th 1944.

Close, Joseph H., Spr.;
Age 24. No known grave.

Rogers, William J.R., Spr.;
Age 29. Was killed on September 19th 1944. No known grave.

Trouse Robert G.W., Spr.;
Age 23. Was killed on September 19th 1944. No known grave.

Cottle, Arthur A. Spr.;
Age 25. Was killed on September 20th 1944. No known grave.

Pink, Henry A., Cpl.;
Age 20. Was killed on September 20th 1944.

Gwilliam, Gilbert R.J., Dvr.;
Age 23. Was killed on September 21st 1944.

Morris, Thomas O., Spr.;
Age 25. Was killed on September 21st 1944.

Kelly, John M. Spr.;
Age 25. Was killed on September 23rd 1944.

Ryder, James G., L/Sgt.;
Was killed on September 23rd 1944.

Binyon, Roger B. Captain;
Age 30. Was killed on September 24th 1944. No known grave.

Lawson, Alec, Spr.;
Age 24. Was killed on September 24th 1944.

Snow, Henry E., S/Sgt.;
Age 25. Was killed on September 24th 1944.

Ashworth, Norman B., Cpl.;
Age 25. Was killed on September 25th 1944.

Clarke, Kenneth, Spr.;
Age 24. Was killed on September 24th 1944.

Evans, Robert F.E., Cpl.;
Age 26. Was killed on September 25th 1944.

May, George H. Spr.;
Age 22. Was killed on September 25th/26th 1944.

Shelley, Louis F. Spr.;
Age 30. Was killed on September 25th 26th 1944.

Everitt, John, Spr.;
Age 23. Died as a POW on November 29th 1944.

Turton, Bernard E., Spr.;
Age 25. Listed as dead on April 22nd 1945. No known grave.

Left: Photo taken by Philip Reinders

A Long Tradition

Roll: 9th (Airborne) Field Company, Royal Engineers

GC = killed in glider crash, KIA = killed in action, MIA = missing in action,
POW = prisoner of war, R = returned, UNK = unknown

HQ Platoon:		Sap. D.E. Holtham	GC
Major J.C. Winchester	R	Sap. A. Cuthbertson	GC
Capt. P.H. Wetherill	POW	Sap. E.A.S. Davis	GC
Lt. E.G. Wise	POW	Sap. A. Hall	GC
CSM Cousins	UNK	Sap E.E. Sheppard	GC
Sgt. J.B. Asterley	R	Sap. A.R. Street	GC
Sgt. J. Denning	UNK	Sap. C. Turner	GC
Sgt. Green (ACC)	R	Sap. A.G. Watt	GC
M.T. Sgt. K. Hannabus	R	Sap. J. Westfield	GC
M.T. Sgt J Paffett	POW	Sap. J.S. Williamson	GC
S/Sgt APTC H.E. Snow	KIA	L/Sgt J.G. Ryder	KIA
Cpl. V. Bond	UNK	Cpl. J. Wharton	POW
Cpl. K. Leach	POW	Cpl. S. Aldridge	POW
Cpl. A. Winsor	UNK	Cpl. W.C.E. Barber	POW
L/Cpl. Bamforth	POW	L/Cpl M.S. Knight	R
L/Cpl. G. Hallam	POW	L/Cpl J. Sibley	POW
L/Cpl. K. Hartley	POW	L/Cpl W.T.N. Takle	KIA
Sap. L. Bonner	UNK	Sap. A.F. Andrews	POW
Sap. R.H.B. Foster	UNK	Sap. L. Bamforth	UNK
Sap. R.F. Holdstock	KIA	Sap. A. Beardall	POW
Sap. M.W. Knight	UNK	Sap. Burns	UNK
Sap. Musslewhite	UNK	Sap. R. Clark	POW
Sap. G. Robertson	POW	Sap. W. Coleman	POW
Sap. J Saybye	POW	Sap. P. Greig	KIA
Sap. L.E. Shelly	KIA	Sap. F. Howe	POW
Sap. C. Shepherd	R	Sap. W.H.D. Jones	R
Sap. T. Wann	UNK	Sap. J.M. Kelly	KIA
Sap. M.J. White	POW	Sap. R. Kennedy	POW
Dvr. Callis	UNK	Sap. J. Knight	POW
Dvr. W.G. Edwards	POW	Sap. G.H. May	KIA
Dvr. G. Fairs	R	Sap. R. McAndres	POW
Dvr. C.S. Greenwood	POW	Sap. D. Milne	POW
Dvr. R. Jardine	R	Sap. T.O. Morris	KIA
Dvr. W. Martin	POW	Sap. A.G. Pratt	POW
		Sap. A. Price	R
No. 1 Platoon:		Sap. R.H. Reeves	POW
Capt. R.B. Binyon	MIA	Sap. J. Ross	POW
Sgt. A.E. Oakley	GC	Sap. J. Saunders	R
L/Sgt. R.H. Allen	GC	Sap. W.B. Staniforth	POW
Cpl Arthur L. Clampitt	GC	Sap. A.T. Williams	R
L/Cpl W.H. Burrows	GC	Drv. G. Hudson	POW
L/Cpl Edward Pickburn	GC		
Sap. J.C. Beale	GC	**No. 2 Platoon**	
Sap. C.W. Calvert	GC	Capt. E.C. O'Callaghan	POW
Sap. R. Carney	GC	Lt. R.E.W.J. Timmins	KIA
Sap. J. Evans	GC	Sgt. Dixson	R
Sap. J. Fenyhough	GC	S/Sgt. E.W.S. Gibbons	POW
Sap. E.J. Godfrey	GC	L/Sgt. R.B. Cawood	POW

Cpl. R.F.E. Evans	KIA	Sgt. J.W. Bushell	POW
Cpl A. Lancaster	POW	Sgt. J.H. Telford	POW
L/Cpl. T.P. Bradley	POW	Sgt. D. Wakefield	UNK
L/Cpl. B.V. Burton	R	L/Sgt S. Green	R
L/Cpl. H.S. Carmalt	POW	L/Sgt H. Lake	UNK
L/Cpl. W. Coward	POW	Cpl. N.B. Ashworth	KIA
L/Cpl. W.E. Johnson	POW	Cpl. C.H. Beaver	R
Cpl. W.C. Clifton	POW	Cpl. F. Dennet	UNK
Sap. A. Cameron	POW	Cpl. W.L. Owens	UNK
Sap. T. Carpenter	POW	Cpl. H.A. Pink	KIA
Sap. J.H. Close	MIA	Cpl. L. Raggett	POW
Sap. A.C. Cole	POW	L/Cpl. T. Beveridge	POW
Sap. A.A. Cottle	MIA	L/Cpl. S. Hey	UNK
Sap. E.V. Dane	POW	L/Cpl. J. Hughes	UNK
Sap. J. Everitt	POW	L/Cpl C.W. Wright	POW
Sap. G. Fox	POW	Sap. S. Baker	UNK
Sap. A. Graydon	R	Sap. V. Bamford	UNK
Sap. D. Green	UNK	Sap A.E. Beech	POW
Sap. R. Harvey	POW	Sap. H. Black	R
Sap. A. Hinds	UNK	Sap. W.H. Bowyer	R
Sap. J. Hogg	Pegasus	Sap. J. Boyers	UNK
Sap. T. Hyland	POW	Sap. E. Brookes	POW
Sap. W.H. Knight	POW	Sap. J. Brown	POW
Sap. E. Lindon	POW	Sap. A. Bugden	UNK
Sap. F. Paine	POW	Sap. K. Clarke	KIA
Sap. G. Parkin	POW	Sap. R. Congreave	R
Sap. W.H. Parry	POW	Sap. J. Cook	POW
Sap V.O. Quinton	POW	Sap. J. Ferrier	UNK
Sap. M.W.P. Robinson	POW	Sap. S. Fisher	POW
Sap. W.J.R. Rogers	MIA	Sap. I. Hannabus	R
Sap. R.V. Russell	MIA	Sap. D. Hare	UNK
Sap W.B. Sykes	R	Sap. Henderson	R
Sap. Taylor	R	Sap. Hewlitt	UNK
Sap. H.W. Thompson	POW	Sap. J. Hillman	POW
Sap. E. Thorne	R	Sap Hogan	UNK
Sap. J. Tipler	POW	Sap. J.A. Johnstone	UNK
Sap. R.G.W. Trouse	MIA	Sap. A. Lawson	MIA
Sap. A. Tunningley	POW	Sap. Lewis	UNK
Sap. A. Turner	POW	Sap. McClay	UNK
Sap. R. Turner	POW	Sap. McDonald	UNK
Sap. B.E. Turton	NKG	Sap. McGowan	UNK
Sap. Wheeler	UNK	Sap. G. Miller	R
Sap. C.J. Wilson	POW	Sap. S. Moss	POW
Dvr. J. Donoghue	POW	Sap. R.H. Patterson	POW
Dvr. Marshall	UNK	Sap. Patrick	POW
Dvr. C. Rimes	R	Sap. J. Pedan	POW
Dvr. P.D. Weddell	POW	Sap. C. Postons	POW
Dvr. Young	UNK	Sap. J. Poultney	R
		Sap. D. Rankin	UNK
<u>No. 3 Platoon</u>		Sap. Sampson	UNK
Capt. M. Heggie	POW	Sap. Seymore	UNK
Lt. J. Steel	POW	Sap. W.H. Sherife	POW

Sap. Thompson	UNK
Sap. P. Tighe	UNK
Sap. Todd	UNK
Sap R. Wainwright	UNK
Sap. R. White	UNK
Sap. W. Whiteside	UNK
Sap. C.R. Williams	POW
Sap. W.H.B. Wilson	POW
Sap. J. Young	R
Drv. E. Cordell	UNK
Drv. G.R.J. Gwilliam	KIA

Unknown

Sap. A. Beaumont	UNK
Dvr. K. Mercer	UNK
Sgt. Gisbourne	UNK
Dvr J. Brookfield	UNK
Sap. L Buckley	POW
Sgt. Craig	UNK
Sap. Cridge	UNK
Sap. Duckers	POW
Sap. H. Duckworth	POW
Cpl. E.E.R. Harris	POW
Sap. D. Shaw	R

References:

Primary:

War Diary 9th (Airborne) Field Company, Royal Engineers September 1944
Report: Lessons From Arnhem by Lt-Col. Myers
'The Operations Of 1 Airborne Division At Arnhem September 1944' in
    'Royal Engineer Battlefield Tour'
Account: Major Winchester
Account: Captain O'Callaghan
Account: Barber
Account: Burton
Account: Cawood
Account: Tom Carpenter
Account: Foster
Account: Jardine
Account: Johnson
Account: Major Perkins
Account: Poultry
Account: Ragget
Account: Milne
Account: Sheppard
Account: Thorne
Account: Wann
Account: A.T. Williams
Report of Activities 9 Field Company RE: Winchester
Report: Thompson
Interview of Sapper Knight by Barry Dougherty at Hartenstein 2004
Citation For D.C.M: Sgt. Lake
Citation For Military Medal: Fairs
'A Drop Too Many' by Major-General John Frost
'An Image Of War' by Mark Henniker

Secondary:

'Roll Of Honour Battle Of Arnhem' by J.A. Hey
'Operation Market-Garden Then And Now' by Karel Margry
'Royal Engineer Battlefield Tour: The Seine To The Rhine: Vol. 1' Feb.
    1947
'The History Of The Corps Of Royal Engineers Vol. IX'
'Arnhem 1944:The Airborne Battle' by Martin Middlebrook
'A Bridge Too Far' by C. Ryan 1st Edition 1974
'German Armored Units At Arnhem September 1944' by Marcel Zwarts
'SS Panzer - Aufklarungs - Abteilung 9 And The Arnhem Road Bridge'
    By Marcel Zwarts
'Wings Of The Wind' a novel by Peter Stainforth
'Retake Arnhem Bridge' by Bob Gerritsen and Scott Revell
'Airborne Engineers: The Shiny 9th' by Patrick Pronk
'The 9th' by Tom Purves

Index

1st Battalion, The Border Regt.; 29, 32
1st Indp. Polish Para. Bde.; 37, 39, 40
1st Para. Sqn., RE; 7, 18, 20, 26, 24, 40, 43
4th Para. Sqn. RE; 26, 36, 40
9th Field Company, R.E.:
    HQ; 7, 10, 12, 14, 26
    No. 1 Platoon; 4, 7, 12, 14, 16, 18, 24, 26, 40
    No. 2 Platoon; 4, 7-9, 12-19, 22, 25, 27, 28, 49, 50
    No. 3 Platoon; 4, 5, 7, 12, 14, 18, 19, 24, 30, 33, 40
261st Field Park Coy. RE; 7, 9, 23, 39
299 Sqn. RAF; 9

Barber, Cpl. William; 5, 40, 47
Beandall, Spr.; 37
Beaver, Spr.; 12
Beech, Spr.; 37
Bicycles; 4, 17, 22
Binyon, Capt. R.B.; 4, 12-14, 26, 36, 41
Bridges:
    Railroad; 7, 8, 13, 15, 16, 25
    Road; 8, 17, 18, 20-22, 26, 27, 30, 33, 49
    Pontoon; 8, 16, 17
Brown, Capt.; 39
Burton, L/Cpl. Basil; 43, 44, 45

Carpenter, Spr. Tom; 9, 10, 15, 17, 20, 21, 28, 30, 33
Cawood, L/Sgt. R.O.; 31, 32
Clarke, Spr.; 45
Clarke Crawler; 7
Close, Spr.; 28
Congreave, Spr.; 39
Cook, Spr. J.; 22
Cormie, Capt.; 43
Cottle, Spr. A.A.; 31, 32, 33
Coword, L/Cpl.; 21
CRE; 7, 16, 22, 30, 36, 37, 42
    (also see Myers)

Dane, Spr.; 36
Dorsets; 42
Dover, Major V.; 16

Evans, Cpl.; 28

Fairley, John; 13
Fairs, Dvr. George; 12, 41
Foster, Spr. Raymond H.; 12, 40
Frost, Lt-Col. John; 16, 20, 29, 49

George, Capt.; 43
Gibbons, Sgt. "Sonny"; 20, 30

Glider #383; 10
Glider #385; 10
Glider #386; 10
Glider #389; 9
Glider #390; 9
Graebner, SS-Capt.; 20, 21
Green, Capt. Adjt. RE; 30
Green, L/Sgt.; 36, 40
Greig, Spr.; 12, 14, 25

Hannibus, Spr. I.; 5
Hallum, L/Cpl.; 23
Heggie, Capt. M..; 4, 12, 13, 18, 22, 30, 32, 34
Henniker, Lt-Col. Mark; 45
Hevendorp Ferry; 7, 26, 30, 42, 43, 49
Hey, Cpl.; 26
Hibbert, Major J.A.; 16
Holdstock, Spr.; 10
Hyland, Spr. Tom; 16

Jardine, Dvr. R.; 10
Johnson, L/Cpl. Edwin; 25, 30, 34

Kenny, Spr.; 37
Knight, Spr. Morris; 23, 35
Kraft; 13

Lake, L/Sgt. Hugh; 32, 33, 37, 39, 45
Lancaster, Cpl. A.A.; 30, 34
Lawson, Alec; 35, 41
Livesey, Capt.; 20
Lonsdale Force; 22, 49

Martin, Spr.; 37
May, Spr. 45
Miller, Sgt.; 12
Milne, Spr.; 45
Murray, Major; 17
Myers, Lt-Col. Edmund; 7, 14, 17, 22, 23, 36, 45

Kelly, Spr. John; 40

O'Callaghan, Capt. E.C.; 4, 12, 13, 16-18, 20, 21, 28-31, 33, 34, 49
Operation Freshman; 3, 48

Paffet, Sgt.; 12, 23
Pedan, Spr. 36
Perkins, Major; 24, 26, 36
Pink, Cpl.; 22, 32, 33
Poultney, Spr. J.; 32, 34

Radio(s); 4, 10, 13, 25
Raggett, Cpl. L. 33, 36, 47

Recce Sqn.; 7, 12, 13, 22
Robinson, Spr.; 12, 36
Rogers, Spr. 28
Russell, Spr.; 28
Ryder, L/Sgt. James; 40

Seaborne Tail; 4, 47
Seymour, Clarke, 33
Shepard, Spr.; 13, 41
Snow, PTI Sgt.; 41
Sonnenberg; 24, 25, 29, 40, 49
South Staffordshire Regt.; 22, 26, 32
Steel, Lt. J.; 14, 18, 25
Storrs, Lt.; 36

Tackle, L/Cpl. William; 14, 25

Thomas, Lt.; 43
Thompson, Spr. Harry; 21
Thorne, Spr. E.; 14
Timmins, Lt.; 12, 14, 18
Trouse, Spr. Robert; 21

Wann, Spr. Donald; 45
Weddell, Spr. Danny; 20
Wetherill, Capt. P.H.; 4, 36
William, Spr. A.T.; 12, 14, 42
William, Spr. C.R.; 32
Wilson, Spr. W.H.; 32
Winchester, Major J.C.; 4, 7, 12, 13, 18, 22, 24-26, 29, 35-37, 39-44, 46
Wise, Lt. E.G.; 4, 12, 13, 18, 23

About The Author

John Sliz became fascinated with Operation Market Garden after he read, 'A Bridge Too Far' at the age of nine. A visit to Arnhem in the summer of 2001 only added fuel to the fire, eventually resulting in the publication of his first book, 'The Storm Boat Kings'. While researching this book and waiting for its publication, he wrote a small booklet on the engineer equipment that was used during the operation. 'Engineer Assault Boats In Canadian Service' was published in December 2006.

Since then he has written the first six books of the Market Garden Engineer Series. He currently lives in Toronto, Ontario and is busy researching engineers in World War II. For more information or to contact him please visit: www.stormboatkings.ca

Other Books By The Same Author

By Vanwell Publishing: (www.vanwell.com)
The Storm Boat Kings: The 23rd Royal Canadian Engineers At Arnhem 1944

By Service Publications: (www.servicepub.com)
Non-Bailey Bridging In Canadian Service
Engineer Assault Boats In Canadian Service

Market Garden Engineer Series: (www.stormboatkings.ca)
#1) The Wrong Side Of The River: The Polish Engineer Company At Arnhem
#2) Basic Function: The 4th Parachute Squadron, Royal Engineers At Arnhem
#3) Engineers At The Bridge: The 1st Parachute Squadron Royal Engineers At Arnhem
#4) Assault Boats On The Waal: The 307th Engineer Battalion During Operation Market Garden
#5) Bridging Hell's Highway: The 326th Engineer Battalion During Operation Market Garden